CW00796828

The Atmospheric Western

George Heiron's
evocative photographs

described by
Leslie Price

The
· Transport ·
Treasury

Copyright: Images George Heiron / Transport Treasury, text: Leslie Price.

ISBN: 978-1-913251-06-2

First Published in 2020 by Transport Treasury Publishing Ltd. 16 Highworth Close, High Wycombe, HP13 7PJ

www.ttpublishing.co.uk

Printed in the UK by Henry Ling Limited, at the Dorset Press, Dorchester, DT1 1HD.

Dedication

This work is dedicated to my wife, Patricia, without whose love,
encouragement and support the book would never have been completed.

Acknowledgements

In acknowledgement one has to take account of inspiration; which here is due to all the railwaymen
and women whose contribution to the cohesion and development of the nation and its economic
prosperity for more than a century and a half, more specifically through two world wars, is not
generally recognised. Those who kept the wheels turning enabled the country to keep going right
through to the 1960's. It has also allowed me to express my love and gratitude to my parents
Tom and Hilda, who both imbued in me a love of railways. Tom served for fifty years, joining the
newly formed LMS at Whitchurch, Shropshire, as a lad porter in 1924. During the half century
that followed he dedicated his life to the railway, retiring as a Passenger Guard based at
Shrewsbury, on his sixty fifth birthday in 1974. On the production side I shall forever be
grateful to the late Tony Atkins, a much loved and greatly missed friend and neighbour, who
introduced me to Kevin Robertson the guide and mentor for this book. On the technical side
I am greatly indebted to Andrew Royle at 'The Transport Treasury' who spent considerable
time trawling through Heiron negatives in pursuit of further information as well as supplying
his own observations. There is also Gerry Nichols, Librarian of the Stephenson Locomotive Society,
who added invaluable information regarding the photograph of the
'Cornish Riviera Express', off route, emerging from Box Middle Hill Tunnel (Image No. 35).
Finally we must not forget George Heiron himself, for having the foresight to record the images.

Biography

Les Price was born into a railway family in Shrewsbury in 1945. His father and two uncles
were all 'railway servants' - as the term was then deemed. After starting his career in London
in 1962, he followed his forbears on to the railway at Crewe in 1976, serving in the railway
environment, at various locations, for twenty five years, until retirement in 2002.
During this time he became well aware of the vagaries of life on the railways.

Front cover :

I saw a train at Sapperton Tunnel,
billowing steam from copper capped funnel.
From Brimscombe to summit the valley to climb,
the gradient against her but running on time
'Avondale Castle' working hard
slackening speed with every yard.
Fireman shovelling to keep up steam,
crew and engine a consummate team.
In smoke and darkness soon consumed;
for eight more furlongs so entombed.
GH152.

Title page:

Vignette of County 4-6-0 No. 1018
'County of Leicester' at Bristol Temple Meads soon after nationalisation and lettered 'British Railways' on the tender.
GH1139.

Rear cover: GH041

The semaphore signals stand silent; the tracks are deserted. The steam engines have gone. All this was encapsulated in Caryl Brahms poem featured on 'That Was The Week That Was' (TW3), a BBC TV satirical Current Affairs programme transmitted the day after the publication of the Beeching Report in 1963.

Old engines with their primal anger gone
Their fire and fury rusted quite away
No longer chuffing into Platform 1
Butchered to make a scrap yard's holiday
Don't think they will not take it hard at Hatch
Thornfalcon, Donyatt, Chard, their summary despatch

Below:

'King' No. 6001 'King Edward V11' awaits departure from Paddington. GH50.

INTRODUCTION

George Heiron was one of the leading railway photographers of his generation. He ranked alongside such renowned names as Eric Treacy, W.J. V. Anderson, R.E. Vincent and R. C. Riley among many others. Indeed such was his standing that he and Eric Treacy produced a book of their combined works, 'Steam's Indian Summer', published by George Allen & Unwin in 1979. But there was one other thing which made George stand apart; he was an accomplished artist in his own right; arguably among the best of railway artists of his generation. His output was also prodigious.

George was the consummate railway photographer with a number of his photographs used as the basis for some of his paintings. He was able to use his skill to construct his photographs with an artistic eye - as will be seen in many of the pictures in this book. They were as often composed by placing a train into the landscape as they were by simply focusing on the train itself. He also had the particular ability and foresight for the time in being able to take photographs in all conditions, all seasons and during the dark hours or in daylight. He turned out come rain, shine or snow as will be well illustrated here. Personally, I particularly savour a picture which tells a story and this is where George excelled.

We should be grateful to people like George who coincidentally recorded social scenes during a time now past. By recording station views and other aspects of railway operations he was, whether by design or not, simultaneously recording the social history of the period. George was a 'Bristolian' and so the majority of the photographs seen in the pages that follow were taken within a thirty to forty miles radius of the city, most of which were reached on his trusty bicycle. Other locations further afield would involve an actual train journey.

Whilst this is a book aimed primarily at the enthusiast, it is also a look back over the shoulder to what is now a bygone era. A reminder of where we came from and how quickly time has moved on. The decade in which it is set, the 1950's into 1960's was the birth and early growth of the second Elizabethan age, resulting in the final development of steam locomotives and the peak of the steam age on the railways.

Regrettably this peak was short-lived to be hastily followed by the sudden decline and fall of steam together with its ultimate elimination. Indeed many steam engines built in the 1950s had a life span of ten years or less. Fortunately there were some brilliant photographers at the time to record these never to be forgotten times. None was more expert than George Heiron.

As a young boy during that era, I lived in a house which backed on to a main railway line in the northern outskirts of Shrewsbury. I would fall asleep to the sound of the Swansea-York mail. Headed by a Stanier 'Coronation Pacific', it quietly padded its way up Crewe Bank out of town before emerging from beneath a farm overbridge just before the house. In a crescendo of sound it then stormed away over Harlescott Crossing and beyond; forging its way further up the bank towards Battlefield and onward to Crewe; the sound continuing to resonate in my ears as it faded into the distance. William Stanier, of course, was Swindon born and had trained at the Great Western Works.

In this way steam was impressed into my psyche. To me journeying by train was the only way to travel; it was a time when coal was the lifeblood of the nation and the railways were the vessels that carried it. It was also the way I was first introduced to George's photographs through journals such as 'Trains Illustrated' and the 'Railway Magazine'.

I now feel privileged, having been invited to both select and caption some of the photographs of a man who to many was arguably one of the foremost exponents of railway photography of his time. To those of my generation this book will be pure nostalgia. To following generations, our children and grandchildren, it will be a view into the early life and times of their parents and forebears. Hopefully too this will bring a new perspective to George's work.

Although several of his photographs may already have been previously published, I have attempted here to select as many as possible which have not. A general reference to publications in which some have appeared is printed at the end of the book. There may be others. However the 21st century has given us a further advantage in that printing techniques have improved beyond what could ever have been imagined 50+ years ago when the first of George's images graced the pages of books and magazines.

So let me take you on a journey with George. It starts at the seaside just south of Bristol and we travel up to London via Bath. After a short stay at Paddington we retrace our tracks back to Swindon and then take the route via Sapperton down the beautiful Gloucestershire Golden Valley to Gloucester itself. From here we backtrack to Standish Junction and on to the old Gloucester and Bristol Railway of 1844 down to Yate and Westerleigh. Then it is back towards Swindon via Hullavington, in order to pick up the 1903 South Wales Direct main line through Badminton, in order to continue our onward journey west into Wales. We go through to Cardiff before returning to Bristol by the same route as far as Filton Junction. In this very convoluted way we arrive back at Temple Meads to witness the elimination of steam and the changing face of the railways as we knew them, to the diesel precursors of what we have today.

I very much hope you enjoy the journey.

Les Price

Inkpen, West Berkshire , August 2019.

Image 1: We begin our journey at the seaside, Weston-super-Mare to be precise; a Restaurant-Car express stands alongside Platform 1. Has the train just arrived? Are the holiday makers coming or going? From the emptiness of the train and the calmness of the passengers on the platform it is rather the former that is suggested. It appears to be a high summer day and George has fully captured the atmosphere of English holidays in the late 50s/early60s period. Trilby's and flat caps are de rigueur as the standard gentleman's headwear and the older generation are attired in coats and jackets. The Platform Inspector deals with an enquiry while two young mothers walk towards the camera, one in a summer frock the other in light jumper and slacks. They both appear to have back-combed bouffant hair styles, a fashion feature of the day as was the shift dress. Note also the pushchairs; rather more simplistic than those which might be expected today. GH744.

Image 2, above: The Portishead Branch joined the main line at Bedminster Junction just north of which was the Bristol suburban station of Bedminster. From Bedminster Park looking towards that station on a warm summer day, a well turned out Hawksworth 'County' No. 1014 'County of Glamorgan' drifts past Bedminster signal box, opposite the park, towards Temple Meads. Train Reporting No. '263' was the 8am Plymouth to Crewe express. Throughout the decade Bedminster Box was open continuously, twenty four hours a day. Note the signalman has already returned the semaphores to the 'on' position after the passage of the locomotive (or were they track-circuit controlled?) and now stands back from his open window observing the train. In front of the box are the buffer stops of the head shunt for Pylle Hill Goods Depot. The prominent building in the background behind the signal box is the colour printing works of E.S. & A Robinson built in 1887. Although no longer owned by the company the five storey factory building still stands and has been developed into residential apartments. GH1049.

Image 3, left: As we travel into Bristol time is taken out for a short trip down the Portishead branch line which clings to the southern bank of the River Avon just west of Brunel's Clifton Suspension Bridge dominating the background. The tide is out exposing the river's mudflats. An ex-GWR Railcar is working a Bristol Temple Meads to Portishead service. Beneath Leigh Woods, a National Trust property, from which the photograph was taken, some 200 feet above river level, two young boys greet its passage. These Railcars were first introduced in 1933 and became nicknamed 'flying bananas' because of their original colour and appearance. Passenger services were withdrawn from the branch in 1964 but a plan to reopen the line, backed by all relevant local councils, is now at an advanced stage. GH022.

Image 4: When George turned his camera around to face north this is the view he obtained. Bedminster Park was the perfect location to sit and watch the trains go by. From here one could watch all the comings and goings between Temple Meads and the west and George has captured this perfectly. The train and two sets of original Great Western wooden-post semaphore signals are beautifully framed by a pair of trees bearing their springtime foliage; it must be May? A 'Grange' Class 4-6-0 No. 6824 'Ashley Grange' breezes west with, according to its headlamp code, an ordinary passenger train. 'Ashley Grange' was a Penzance (83G) based locomotive so she is obviously in the course of working her way back home on this passenger; probably not all the way, possibly either Exeter or more likely Plymouth. To the rear of the train is Pylle Hill Goods Depot in front of which stands the water tower from which engines could replenish their supply before setting out. GH1050.

Image 5: A panoramic view of south-west Bristol from an elevated position; looking across to Pylle Hill Depot and beyond. With the backdrop of a very neat and tidy goods depot a 'County' Class 4-6-0 runs the last couple of chains to Temple Meads with an eight coach express from the west. It is met by a Beyer Peacock (Hymek) Type 3 Diesel Hydraulic D7018 heading west with a passenger train. The Hymeks, introduced in 1961, were soon to displace engines such as the 'County' Class who were now living on borrowed time on the Western. Note too, the progress in freight movement in the Depot with the introduction of 'first-generation' container traffic. This was the initial stage in road/ rail development with here the containers conveyed on either flat-bed trucks or even within five plank wagons. In the distance a train is about to leave Bedminster station on the slow line. **GH1028.**

Image 6: And so to Temple Meads, Brunel's other masterpiece in Bristol. It is a busy summer Saturday morning at the west end of the station. The late 1950s was when holidays to the West Country peaked and most people still travelled by train. Many additional services were put on to carry them and Bristol was at the centre of activities. As several of these trains did not carry buffet cars an extended stop was made here in order that passengers could use the station facilities. For this purpose Refreshment Rooms were provided on Platforms 3-4/5 on the 'Down' side and similarly Platforms 6/7 on the 'Up' side. A number of people are also seen milling around on the platform taking the opportunity to stretch their legs during the break in their journey. Meanwhile 'Britannia' Class Pacific No. 70028 'Royal Star' pulls out of Platform 2 with a heavily loaded train. It is impossible to say what her destination is as the train reporting frame has been left blank although the **Class B** headlamp code (one lamp atop the smokebox) tells us it is merely an ordinary passenger train. Behind her two further trains wait. The one in Platform 4 is headed by a 'Castle' carrying reporting number '107'. This was the 7.30am Paddington to Paignton which ran every weekday during the summer. A 'Hall' with train '815', the 6.55am Saturdays only Wolverhampton to Paignton, stands alongside Platform 5. **GH1109.**

Image 7: 'Trouble with the points' could well be the title of this photograph. The leading coach of the train is a Churchward designed 'toplight', a name derived from the small windows adjacent to the ventilators towards the roof of the coach. Given that the 'Britannias' were not introduced on to the Western Region until 1951 this must be a very early decade Heiron photograph because of the age of this coach. George captures yet another aspect of railway operations, this time the permanent way. But he frames it very appealingly to add more interest. A westbound express, headed by a 'Castle' in tandem with a 'Britannia', moves vigorously west out of Platform 4 at Temple Meads with a late summer evening express. Under the scrutiny of a man, who is probably a Permanent Way Supervisor, carrying a manual and some kind of key behind his back, they head towards the sunset. Further to the right two men attend to the job in hand, the mechanism powering the points at the adjacent platform. A 'lookout' on the extreme right *(the view has not been cropped)* keeps his eye out for any approaching traffic. The photograph highlights two significant facts, the first; the railways run 24 hours a day and the second, in the days of steam, they were very labour intensive. Beneath the girder bridge carrying the A4 road across the tracks may be seen Bristol West Signal Box, the counterpart to Bristol East at the other end of the station. GH1122.

Image 8: It was the high level of activity which attracted the train spotters; a picture which perfectly illustrates the favourite pastime of young boys of a certain generation. A gaggle has assembled at the west end of Platforms 4 and 5. From here the best view was also afforded of the activities on Bath Road shed opposite the station, hence the concentration of train spotters. They always felt at home milling about on platform ends to the extent that in this case, one has even sat down and is seen dangling his legs over the platform edge. Not only a very dangerous action but if caught could result in him (and even his colleagues) all being thrown off the station or despatched home on the next available train. Some are checking their books to see if they have 'copped' the Hawksworth 'County' which is just running in 'Up' Platform 8. Also in the picture a 'Pannier' tank tends to some parcel vans whilst what appears to be a '45xx' tank moves light engine, through the station. You might say the pigeons in the bottom right hand corner have a birds-eye view. GH1115.

Image 9: Possibly the view those train spotters may have been looking at; arguably the Western's most iconic locomotive, Collett's 'King' Class 4-6-0 No. 6000 'King George V'. Here she is reposing on Bristol (Bath Road) shed between duties. It was this engine which first inspired George's interest in railways when his mother took him to Temple Meads to watch trains; to quote, "It all took off from there". During the 1950s 'KGV' was based at Old Oak Common (81A) and spent her working life mostly heading famous named trains to 'The West'. Intriguingly the head board she carries here has been turned back to front whilst she is on shed. It looks suspiciously like the 'Merchant Venturer' which ran between Paddington and Weston-super-Mare - and return. 'KGV' was out-shopped from Swindon in June 1927 and after being 'run-in' it was shipped to America to take part in the centenary celebrations of the Baltimore and Ohio Railway. During these celebrations it was presented with a bell as seen on the front buffer beam and plaque to commemorate the event. The engine is certainly ready for 'the off' with her safety valve blowing wildly and the fireman looking out expectantly for the signal. She is amongst lesser mortals being serviced; a '53xx' Class 2-6-0 beside her, and behind a 'Hall' with a 'Castle' being coaled beyond. GH1017.

Image 10: A superb all-encompassing view of Bristol (Bath Road) (82A) shed taken from the same platform end. According to the shed clock it is 2.55pm and a good range of 'Western' engines are on show. With her safety valve blowing, a visitor, '49xx' 4-6-0 No. 4956 'Plowden Hall' is ready to move off. For a period in the middle of the decade No. 4956 was a Cardiff (Canton) (86C) based engine and, since she has been set up with a Class 'B', ordinary passenger head code, is probably ready to work an intermediate stopping train back to her home. There is a fine array of engines from humble tanks to main line locomotives on view: from left to right a 2-6-2 Tank, a 'Hall' and a '94xx Class' 0-6-0 PT beside the coaling stage. Moving across to the main shed another 0-6-0PT and a variety of other 'ex Great Western' types may be seen before we come to a 'Castle' displaying Train Reporting No. '825', together with a headboard. The reporting code referred to the 9am Wolverhampton –Penzance, 'The Cornishman', scheduled to arrive at Bristol at 12.15pm. If this was a Wolverhampton (Stafford Road) (84A) engine then she would have been turned on arrival and undergone servicing before working the return, which on weekdays left Bristol at 4.8pm. That being the case her return reporting number has yet to be changed. GH1023.

Image 11: From the same position an almost identical shot as the previous picture, but this time a nocturnal view. At night the railways took on another aura; half a century ago they were a completely different entity to the modern railway. It has to be remembered, during the night hours a vast quantity of freight, better known then as simply 'goods', was carried by rail. Road haulage, whilst a growing competition to rail, did not have the benefit of the modern motorway network hence rail was still the preferred option for most. In addition telephone communications were still not widespread and most people did not have a landline at home. Consequently the principal means of communication was the letter or humble postcard with countless thousands of smaller items by the Post Office parcel. Into this context we must place the railways with most goods and mail traffic, not to mention some passenger trains, travelling overnight. Engine sheds, here illustrated by Bath Road depot, make the point that railways were as busy at night as by day. It is 7.15pm on a winter evening and the shed lights illuminate the black sky. Some engines are being serviced and others are ready for the road. GH1026.

Image 12: The much sought after picture by any railway photographer, two trains meeting on adjacent tracks. Here, by quirk of fate, the timing could not have been bettered. 'Grange' Class No. 6814 'Enborne Grange', still in post-war **GWR** livery, drifts into one of the 'Up' platforms at Temple Meads with her driver looking steadfastly forward checking his approach. During the early part of the decade '6814' was a Newton Abbot (83A) engine so likely the train would have originated on the Torbay line. Above the locomotive's exhaust the parcel bays are full of vans and goods are piled high on the platform, keeping the porters busy. Meanwhile on the 'Down' side a 'Hall' displaying train reporting code '100' is pulling out of Platform 4. From the summer of 1952 through to summer 1957 this train ran as the 5.30am (**SX**) Paddington - Penzance, the destination being changed to Minehead via Bristol on Saturdays only. Perhaps this is the Saturday train we are looking at? Certainly in days of yore holiday makers rose early to go on holiday whilst it is also probably fair to say they couldn't arrive at their chosen destination soon enough. GH1118.

Image 13: Photographed coming off shed at Bath Road and moving forward towards the east end of the station. This is 'Britannia' No. 70028 'Royal Star'; from new in October 1952 it was sent to Cardiff (Canton) (86C) where it remained allocated right through the decade until September 1961. This may give a clue as to the destination of the train it is going to pick-up. Note the slack pipe draped out of the cab side window, it was used to wet down the coal dust on coal in the tender and generally hose the footplate to keep it clean. The name slack pipe was derived from the nutty slack that the engine often had for coal, slack being a word meaning coal dust or small pieces of coal; derived from this came the term 'to slake' meaning 'to lay down dust'. GH1108.

Image 14: Above: Evening at Temple Meads and here we have a picture which may forever remain a conundrum! 'Hall' Class No. 6997 'Bryn -Ivor Hall' stands on the downside in Platform 4. As its shed plate code shows it was a Bath Road based engine. So it is standing in its home station with Train Reporting Number 'B11' chalked on its smoke box door. In the winter timetable for 1960 this number referred to the 1.15pm Paddington to Weston-super-Mare express, due Bristol at 3.15pm. However the clock on the almost deserted platform shows the time to be 8.40pm on a dark evening so it could not possibly be this train. Perhaps the engine had been rostered for a further service without the reporting number being removed? GH 61.

Image 15: Left: Perhaps in readiness to work an express forward to Paddington 'Castle' Class No. 7018 'Drysllwyn Castle' comes off her home shed at Bath Road. This locomotive had a short but illustrious career. Built at Swindon in May 1949 to Lot No. 367, she quickly gained a reputation as a mediocre steamer. This photograph was taken subsequent to May 1956 after she had been recalled to Swindon for modification to be fitted with an experimental twin blast-pipe and a double chimney. Here she is seen also coupled to a self-weighing tender. The mechanical changes effected transformed the previous lack-lustre machine so much that a further 66 'Castles' were subsequently altered in the same way. Later on in April 1958 she was again returned to Swindon this time to be fitted with a four-row superheater and other minor modifications. After being out-shopped she went back to Bath Road and was put to work on the 'Bristolian'. In the same month she took the train the 117 miles to Paddington in 93 minutes 50 seconds, recording a top speed of 100mph at Little Somerford. It was a record run for the 'Bristolian'. Unfortunately this claim to fame was not enough to earmark her as one of the 'Castles' to survive into preservation. She was withdrawn in September 1963 and went to Cashmore's at Great Bridge in Birmingham, there to be reduced to scrap. GH 1140.

Image 16: George was just as good a social historian as he was an expert railway photographer. To him the people using the railway were just as important a component of the scene, as the locomotives and train themselves. This is clearly displayed in the view of passengers milling around at the top of the flight of stairs leading down to the subway from platforms 1 and 2. The clock tells us it is just after midday. The paper label in the carriage window indicates the train has just arrived and appears to be terminating. Some people are pondering where to go next on this busy station; those in the know head straight for the steps. The scene is very redolent of its period and the passengers are dressed in their summer travelling clothes. Note the serviceman in his blouson jacket with kitbag thrown over his shoulder. Of particular interest is the young lady carrying her coat and handbag safely secured in a straw tote bag in one hand and suitcase in the other. Her skirt is made from material featuring pictures of the film stars of the day. **GH56**.

Image 17: Three-quarters of an hour before the time shown in the previous photograph, a scene of activity is captured at the other end of the station. Viewed from the eastern end of Platform 2 an immaculate 'County' Class No. 1026 'County of Salop' glistens in the sunlight as she simmers at Platform 7. A host of train spotters look on as both the fireman and a cleaner especially provided from Bath Road are engaged in drawing coal forward on the tender. The leading carriage carries a roofboard 'Plymouth-Crewe-Glasgow'. A glance at the relevant timetable of the period explains that this is the 8am Plymouth to Liverpool and Glasgow. The train was due to arrive at Temple Meads at 11.15am and stood for seven minutes before '1026' resumed its journey back to its home shed at Shrewsbury. As for any Glasgow passengers they could not expect to get home before 10.50pm, a marathon journey of almost fifteen hours from Plymouth, surely one of the longest on the system. What about the man with the dog? I wonder if he told his wife where he was taking it for a walk! 'County of Salop' happened to be my favourite locomotive; well, being a proud Salopian why wouldn't it be? GH1562.

Image 18: Train spotters are out in force at this end of the station too. The centre of attention here being 'The Cornishman'. This train ran on weekdays (Saturday and Sunday excepted) during the summer between Penzance and Wolverhampton (Low Level). It is seen taking its leave from Platform 7 in front of groups of young enthusiasts on each platform. Note the one in front of the camera, taking his own picture, who obviously arrived at the station on his bicycle...... . The locomotive is 'Castle' Class No.5019 'Treago Castle', a Wolverhampton (Stafford Road) (84A) engine from May 1958 until she was withdrawn in September 1962. After the major restructure of train reporting numbers in 1960 the train carried No. 'H32', leaving Penzance on weekdays at 10.30am but on Mondays to Thursdays picking up a portion from Kingswear at Temple Meads. On Fridays only there was no Kingswear portion which resulted in a reduced station time at Bristol and an arrival at Wolverhampton at 7.3pm instead of the other days when it was 7.25pm. **GH51.**

Image 19: Amid lengthening shadows, this is the western end of the station from Platform 4. An unidentified 'Castle', which looks suspiciously like No. 5077 'Fairey Battle', awaits departure with a westbound express. Whilst the driver looks back for 'the tip' from platform staff the fireman busies himself shovelling coal forward in the tender - usually the tender would have been prepared in advance. It appears the locomotive may have just joined the train here because alongside on the platform is a boiler-suited man with his hair covered dressed like a fitter. He may well have come off shed with the engine to check its performance before it sets off. He is slaking his thirst from a mug which he could have filled from the tap attached to the stanchion supporting the platform awning. Also of interest are the mail bags in a pile on the platform. They have perhaps been thrown from the guards van double doors of the **BR Mark 1** coach No. W9273, a **BCK** (Brake corridor composite) or **BSK** (brake corridor second). 'Fairey Battle' was a Bath Road engine from June 1954 to July 1956. It otherwise spent much of the decade operating out of sheds in South Wales.
GH424.

Image 20: Trouble with water at the eastern end of Temple Meads. The driver operating the water column looks on haplessly as the water intended for his 'Prairie' tank engine begins to overflow. Is that his mate running across the tracks to help him? The indication of the headlamp code is that of a light engine but the locomotive appears to be attached to at least one suburban coach. Meanwhile 'County' Class No. 1003 'County of Warwick' which was a long-term Shrewsbury (84G) engine, eases out of platform 9. She was based there from 1951 through to 1961. You may then imagine this was a west to north express but the carriage roof boards state 'Paddington Bath Spa and Bristol', confirming that it is bound for Paddington. She would appear therefore to be heading back to her home shed via a very circuitous route. Steam continues to pour from the safety valves as the driver looks out for the camera before opening up the regulator. GH1609.

Image 21: Above: Viewed from Platform 9; a lady passenger strides from the direction of Platform 12, in the old part of the station, towards the subway with handbag and umbrella in one hand and suitcase in the other. The picture captures the whole railway scene of the period. Across in Platform 7 'King' Class No. 6027 'King Richard I' awaits departure on a Paddington express, with the fireman getting himself into the picture. But the over-riding feature is how important the railway was to the movement of mail around the country; the barrows are piled high. Such was the volume of mail that at a principal station such as Temple Meads postmen were specifically employed to load and unload mail. This traffic is further emphasised, in the background, by the Travelling Post Office vehicle being stabled, together with a Collett coach, by a 'Pannier Tank' in readiness to be added to an incoming train. GH1589.

Image 22: Left: Nearby, in Brunel's original train shed at Platform 14, stands Ex- GWR Railcar No. W28W; beneath a Signal Box, the nameplate of which reads 'Bristol Old Station Signal Box'. This box was opened on 5th August 1878, the cast iron nameplate being ordered from Reading in 1898. It ceased to operate on 12th September 1965 when these platform lines closed, except for a small section of Platform 12 that became controlled from Bristol East Box. By now well over twenty years old, these GWR Railcars carried out sterling work right through to the 1960s. W28W entered service in 1940 and was withdrawn in the first years of the 1960s after work on a range of suburban services in the Bristol area. GH1579.

Image 23: A general view of the two main 'Up' departure platforms. In each of his compositions George is able to illustrate so much period detail. For example this picture demonstrates that, for train crews, there were as many periods of relaxation as there were of intense activity and hard physical work. On the left of the picture we see a footplate man draped over the platform end barrier eating his paper wrapped portion of chips. Meanwhile in the shadow of the train on the left two other train crew have taken their seating on point rodding, awaiting the locomotive to take their train forward from Platform 7. A third has settled himself on the step of the leading carriage. Sitting in Platform 9 'Castle' Class No.5078 'Beaufort' awaits departure with train 'A43'. When the new train reporting codes were introduced in the summer of 1960, this was allocated to the weekday 11.45am Temple Meads-Paddington. 'Beaufort', at this time was a Bath Road engine. The coach in Platform 7 is part of an ex-LMS set, with Guard's Brake van end lookout windows that is likely to be forming a return working from the west to northern England. From my own experience I can say it was quite normal for Mum & Dad to take their children to the front of the train to 'see the engine'! GH423.

Image 24: George, standing at the head of Platform 3, has now turned his camera round to record the departure of a Paddington express, the formation of which is a Hawksworth coach immediately behind the tender followed by a Churchward build and then various Collett vehicles. The engine's exhaust climbs vertically into a pure azure blue sky as it pulls out past Bristol East Power Box . Of course the Second World War had taken a very heavy toll on the railways, when much was expected but little was invested. It was this state of affairs which led to the 'Big Four' being nationalised and it took until 1955 before a plan was proposed to modernise the railways. GH1578.

Image 25: On our way out of Bristol we are treated to a wonderfully panoramic view of Bristol East Yard, possibly the Western Region's principal exchange sidings in Bristol. To the left, in the background is St. Philip's Marsh. By the date this picture was taken these sidings were unquestionably becoming less busy than they had been in former years; many of the lines, particularly on the 'Up' side being devoid of traffic. Nevertheless the yard shunter, a Hawksworth '94xx' Class 0-6-0 Pannier Tank, introduced from 1947, is occupied in the 'Down' yard and a more conventional 'Matchbox' pannier tank brings a transfer freight of wagons loaded with piping from the direction of St. Philip's Marsh. Through this plethora of lines a 'Castle' class engine threads its way towards Temple Meads with a 'Down' express. Much of the Yard was cut out of rock, this photograph being taken from an elevated position on a minor road to the west of St. Anne's Park Station. GH1015.

Image 26: Above: For most trains to Paddington the first call was at Bath and as we run in we see 'Castle' Class No. 5014 'Goodrich Castle' restarting the westbound 'Merchant Venturer' over the arches out of the city. Here the line briefly runs alongside the main A367 road to Wells. The road sign shows us all the routes out of Bath at this point. Note the limited amounts of period traffic, the most prominent vehicle being a Morris Commercial J-Type Van and in the background another popular means of transport; the motorbike and sidecar. 'The Merchant Venturer' was inaugurated at the beginning of May 1951 in conjunction with the 'Festival of Britain'. This must have been another picture taken early in the decade given the mix of rolling stock making up the train. They are primarily Collett and Hawksworth coaches but the third vehicle back is a Churchward 'Toplight'; a design dating back to 1907. As late as 1958 the 'Up' 'Merchant Venturer' also still carried a 'slip-coach' which was detached at Reading. GH787.

Image 27: Left: A panoramic view of St. Annes Park station, with a London bound train disappearing into the tunnel beyond. In the foreground an unidentified double-chimney 'Castle' Class locomotive runs through the station with 'Train 116'. This service was introduced on 16th June 1954 and was the forerunner to the 'high speed', non-stop 'Down' Bristolian' which subsequently cut out the stop at Bath. By the summer of 1955 it had become the fully fledged 'Bristolian' running on a schedule of more than a mile a minute. Thus this picture must have been taken shortly after, particularly given that the coaches appear to be BR Mark 1s. The train was unique in that the 'Up' train climbed Filton bank and ran to Paddington via the Badminton Route (117.6miles) whereas the 'Down' train ran via Brunel's original route through Bath (118.3 miles), both with a 105 minutes schedule for their respective journeys. GH1473.

Image 28: A truly all encompassing view; captured in a portrait totally evocative of its period. Perhaps completely unintended, George has nevertheless captured a prophetic comparison regarding the forthcoming battle between road and rail transport. Here he records the competition between the progressive development of rail transport and that of road, at a time when the latter was increasingly challenging rail. Many will be very interested in the train leaving **Bath Spa**, above the streets, behind the prototype main line gas turbine-electric locomotive **No. 18100**, built for British Railways in 1951 by Metropolitan-Vickers, which spent a very short working life on the Western Region. Here she is heading west with train '142', the 'Merchant Venturer', introduced as the 11.15am from Paddington to Bristol. It was allowed 106 minutes to run the one hundred and seven miles non-stop to Bath where it was due at 1.01pm. After another eleven and a half miles, it was due at Temple Meads at 1.22pm; a very slick schedule. The locomotive worked this train more than it did any other but after repeated problems including excessive fuel consumption its short working life ended when it was taken out of capital service in November 1953. The photograph therefore was taken prior to this; a very early Heiron picture. Some readers may be drawn to the fine variety of motor coaches in the coach park whilst their passengers enjoy a day trip to Bath. **G**H767.

Image 29: At Bathampton Junction, east of Bath, we take time out to travel twenty or so miles to Norton Bavant just beyond Warminster in the Wylye Valley. Here deep in Wiltshire 'Downland' country, we see South Wales based 'Castle' No. 7016 'Chester Castle', cantering east between Warminster and Salisbury at the head of a Class 'B' stopping train. The interesting feature of the eight coach formation is its makeup. Whilst the rear three carriages appear to be of standard ex Great Western origin, the first five are pure ex Southern Railway. During the latter years of the **SR**'s existence Oliver Bulleid designed coaches, many of which were put into sets for ease of maintenance. 'Set 840' became a permanent five car set in autumn 1959 and was painted in Crimson and Cream. It comprised (from the front), **BSK, SK, CK, SK** and **BSK**. This design also led to the development of the nationalised **BR Mark 1 Coach**. The location and formation suggests it is possibly a Bristol or Cardiff to South Coast working. The striking thing about this picture is how pastoral, neat and tidy the scene is with cows quietly grazing in the meadow beyond. A platelayers hut, built from redundant sleepers with its brick chimney, is prominent. The platelayer, a term which goes as far back as the origin of the railways, is now more commonly called a trackman. In those days the platelayer together with the local ganger had the responsibility of inspecting and maintaining the track. The ganger especially was often to be seen walking along his length with a long-handled hammer balanced over his shoulder. When he came across a loose wooden key intended to hold the rail tight in its chair he would use the hammer to knock the key back into place. The name lengthman was another term derived from the canal era, the lengthman, as the name implies, responsible for the up-keep of a certain length of track (or canal). Many covered fairly rural and isolated areas and to enable the permanent way gang to store materials and work through inclement weather such huts, or bothies, were strategically placed along a length to afford shelter and an opportunity to make a hot drink. The engine is just passing over an **ATC** ramp set between the rails and so dependent upon the position of the distant signal (out of view) either a bell or siren will have sounded in the engine cab. (With thanks to Andrew Royle at the Transport Treasury for determining the precise location of this photograph). **GH**117.

Image 30: Back on the mainline, approaching **Box**, is the hamlet of **Shockerwick**. Here a footbridge spans the line and was also one of George's favoured locations. Approaching the footbridge coasting downhill from **Box** is a 'Castle' No. 5062 'Earl of Shaftesbury' at the head of a 'Down' express. Towards the end of the decade she was a Bath Road (82A) based engine so is working home to Bristol. Nowadays this beautiful landscaped view is no longer available. Here the photograph illustrates a couple of cars heading towards Bath on the A4 trunk road; a third, disappearing into the distance. The line side, immaculately maintained sixty years ago, is nowadays totally obscured with trees and vegetation so the road can no longer be seen from the railway. The footbridge still spans the track at the same location and even appears to have been renewed. Similarly the skill and dedication of the lengthman who maintained this scene has passed into history. **GH453.**

Image 31, top: Nearing Box and photographed from the A4 overbridge, '4073 Castle' Class No. 5025 'Chirk Castle' bowls effortlessly along past Shockerwick with the 'Up' 'Merchant Venturer' one summer's evening. Her last call had been at Bath Spa at 5.49pm and her next would be Chippenham at 6.10pm. During the period the photograph was taken, No. 5025 was an Old Oak Common (81A) engine so the likelihood is that she would have worked the 'Down' 'Merchant Venturer' during the morning and was now working her way back home. Note the elevated Box down advanced starting signal necessarily placed on the 'Up' side of the line for visibility purposes as trains raced downhill through Box. It also appears to have lost its finial from the top of the post. On the right of the picture runs the main A4 London to Bath and Bristol road this time with just one vehicle in view. GH1509.

Image 32:, opposite: Taken from the same vantage point but on the opposite side of the bridge; a scene of tranquillity. In the absence of express trains rushing through the station, all that can be heard is the subdued but throaty exhaust of a '6959' series 'Modified Hall' No. 7914 'Lleweni Hall'. Standing in the station with a Swindon to Bristol stopping train, she awaits the 'right-away'. Emitting vertically from its chimney; upright as a flagpole, the smoke dissipates and disappears into the calm summer sky. This class of locomotive was a development of the Collett designed 'Halls' of 1924. In 1944 F. W. Hawksworth introduced engines with larger superheaters, 'one-piece' main frames and a plate framed bogie. The '79xx' type were the ultimate batch of such locomotives to be produced, the first of which was delivered from Swindon under BR ownership in April 1949. Six 'Modified Halls' survive in preservation. GH1525.

Image 33: With the introduction of diesel traction, steam engines began to suffer as a result of less attention. This picture taken from the footbridge looking west exemplifies it. With steam escaping from places it shouldn't, a rather dishevelled 'Castle' lays a thick veil of black smoke over Box station as it climbs the 1 in 100 gradient to Box Tunnel. Not wishing to point a finger but its shed code plate is 82A (Bath Road) and the train it is heading, 'A64', is a Paddington bound express which makes this a post 1959 photograph. Other period details are revealed; the signalman no longer cycles to work; he now possesses a small capacity motor bike. He stops for a chat to his mate before he wends his way home. On the opposite platform tucked under the canopy a four wheeled platform barrow is loaded with mail bags which are either for collection by a postman or have been delivered here for loading onto the next 'Down' local, such as the train in the previous picture. GH1519.

Image 34: Immediately to the east of the station lay Middle Hill Tunnel from above which a panoramic view of the neat layout at Box station was afforded. By virtue of the terrain here the station was located, not very conveniently, at the extreme west end of the village. Viewed from adjacent to the tunnel mouth, the Metropolitan-Vickers Gas Turbine-Electric No. 18000 approaches the station with an express for Bristol. The train has an interesting mix of stock. First behind the locomotive is an ex-LNER 63' 'Thompson' BG (1945) followed by a 'Hawksworth' Brake-3rd Class (1950), then a Collett corridor 3rd (1936) and nearest the camera a Churchward 'Toplight' coach (1922). In the opposite direction a short pick-up goods train approaches the camera. Business for it does not appear to be very brisk with only five open wagons and a 'Toad' brake van behind the 'Prairie' tank engine. GH1505.

Image 35, opposite top: And now a rarity; the 'Down' 'Cornish Riviera Express' races out of Middle Hill Tunnel on a falling gradient behind 'King' No 6027 'King Richard I', a long time Laira (Plymouth) (83D) engine. What is this train doing on the 'Great Way Round', as it was sometimes rather irreverently called, rather than the direct route from Reading to Plymouth? Clearly it has been diverted. Detail modifications on the locomotive indicate that the picture was taken prior to 1953. It has been suggested that it may have occurred sometime between 14th October and 11 November 1951 when the direct route was closed at Patney and Chirton due to extensive engineering works. For that period the weekday 10.30am was diverted via Swindon and Melksham but on Sundays' ran via Bristol. Was this one of those occasions or could it have occurred at another time when engineering works or other problems interfered with normal operations? (With thanks to Gerry Nichols). GH1510.

Image 36, opposite bottom: At the same location is one of the new diesels usurping steam's territory. By now BR Type 4 'Warship' Diesel Hydraulics were increasingly displacing steam engines. Seen here is one of the first three in the class which originally carried short grab handles below each windscreen. D800 'Sir Brian Robertson', introduced in 1958, was the first of its class and named after the Chairman of the British Transport Commission. Given that Train Reporting Numbers were revised for the 1960 summer timetable it is likely this photograph was taken then. Train 'B12' ran seven days a week during that summer from Paddington to Cheltenham & Weston-super-Mare and must have split at Swindon, this being the Weston portion. It had three different departure times from Paddington, 13.38hrs (**SO**), 13.40 hrs (**SX**) and 12.30 (**SuO**). The 'Warships' had a relatively short life all being retired between 1967 and 1972. A total of 76 were built, the first 38 of them at Swindon. Only two survived into preservation, D821 'Greyhound' and D832 'Onslaught'. (With thanks to Andrew Royle.) GH1501.

Image 37 below: Moving further east we now come to Box Tunnel itself. Brunel's calculations were such that the tunnel so aligned with the rising sun visible through it's length on 9th April each year; his birthday. When opened on 30th June 1841 it was the longest railway tunnel in the world. Arguably one of George's best known images, the picture depicts 'King' Class No. 6016 'King Edward V' emerging from the western portal into the daylight. Shown in GWR days and renumbering the engine '6023', George adapted this photograph to use as a painting to adorn the front cover of the book; '*The Great Western Railway: 150 Glorious Years*', published by David and Charles in 1984. GH1513.

Image 38: In the midst of rolling countryside; a superbly composed view taken from the ramparts of Box Tunnel. A spotless 'Castle' No. 4079 'Pendennis Castle' heads towards the western portal with an 'Up' stopping train, probably from Temple Meads to Swindon. Given the condition of the locomotive she could well be on a running-in turn post overhaul and returning to Swindon after a run out on a light passenger train roster. 'Pendennis Castle' was one of the most celebrated locomotives of her Class, completed at Swindon in February 1924. Her claim to fame dates back to 1925 when she was lent to the **LNER** for trials against Nigel Gresley's new Pacifics, exemplified by No. 4472 'Flying Scotsman'. She covered herself in glory completely outperforming her larger competitors. Her exploits led her to being preserved and her subsequent history in preservation is well worth reading. She is now in the loving hands of the **Great Western Society at Didcot.** As for Box Tunnel there is little to be said that is not already known, engineered by Isambard Kingdom Brunel, it ranks alongside the Maidenhead bridge and the Clifton Suspension Bridge as one of his masterpieces. GH1524.

Image 39: Racing through downland countryside we see the 'Merchant Venturer' speeding on its way behind 'Castle' No. 7027 'Thornbury Castle'. From November 1951 to April 1960, she was an **O**ld **O**ak **C**ommon (81A) based engine. Just discernible beyond the train is another line running parallel even so it has not proved possible to confirm the exact location. Recording a train at speed is an art in itself and one fully encompassed by George. It takes a keen eye and a steady hand; especially as George was not given to using a tripod very often. The results, however, could be very rewarding as in this picture that surely depicts the power of steam in all its glory. Technically a panned view is not a simple task; the sweep of the camera must be in total accord with the speed of the train, thus stopping it in focus whilst the background is blurred and the sense of speed so created; but this technique was one of George's many strengths. 'The Merchant Venturer' was inaugurated at the beginning of May 1951, in association with the Festival of Britain, as the 11am to Bristol via Bath. From the outset it ran through to Weston-super-Mare from where it returned at 4.35pm for Paddington. The service ran via Bath in both directions. GH114.

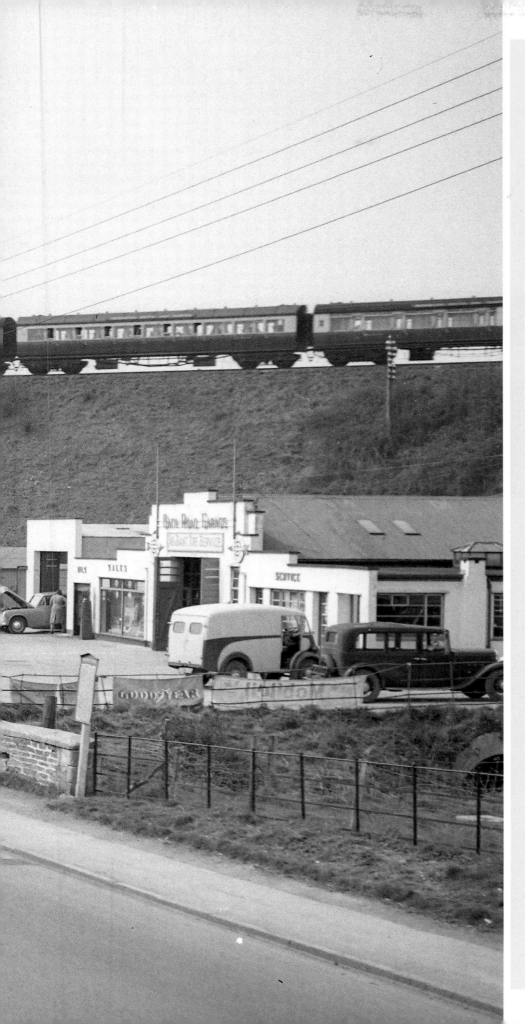

Image 40: We are now approaching Chippenham as an unidentified 'Castle' breezes towards Bristol with a 'Down' express just about to cross the main A4 Bath Road to the west of the town. The locomotive would also appear to be carrying a name board on the front of the smoke box door. The service is made up of ageing stock; Churchward 'Toplights' and a Collett 'high-waist' coach are in view, which would date this from the early to mid-1950s. Note the lack of road competition; only one vehicle can be seen on the main A4. The garage is possibly of more interest in this picture than even the train. On the forecourt no less than five different brands are displayed on the six petrol pumps. These include National Benzole, Esso, Shell, Power and Cleveland. A Hillman Minx is receiving some attention whilst in the foreground is a Morris Commercial J-Type Van and a large saloon car, possibly an Austin. The advertising hoardings are also of interest particularly the Esso one featuring the tiger. From 1959 the slogan 'Put a tiger in your tank' was adopted and became a very successful advertising campaign. But where is everybody; the only people to be seen are the two mechanics attending to the Hillman? GH1469.

Image 41, above: The 'Merchant Venturer' roars through Chippenham behind 'Castle Class' No.7024 'Powis Castle'. The photograph was taken on 8th June 1953; a warm summer day and is very redolent of the period. The train races past the 'running-in board' on the opposite platform, the nearest face of which is the bay for the Calne branch. In similar fashion the consist is almost pure vintage. Four of the first five vehicles of the express are Churchward 57 foot 'Toplight' coaches, the exception is the second coach, a Collett high waist bow-ended coach dating from 1925. In the foreground there seems to be no activity in the goods yard although the doors of the stabled vans are open for loading or unloading. The Great Western 'Toad' brake van in the foreground bears the legend '**CHIPPENHAM R.U.**' 'R.U.' signifies 'restricted use' which means it is for use only locally; possibly restricted to the Calne branch line. **GH**1465.

Image 42: Another early Heiron image with a pair of 3-feet GWR bracket signals on display at Swindon station. In the platform, at the head of an express sits 'Castle' Class No. 5084 'Reading Abbey' under the gaze of an admiring train spotter. By the time of this photograph the engine was over thirty years old and still looking good. Originally built as a member of the 'Star' Class to the design of George Churchward, it was outshopped from Swindon in December 1922 carrying No. 4064. In early 1937 it went back to Works and was rebuilt as a 'Castle', being renumbered '5084' and returning to traffic on 24th March of the same year. Between May 1948 and July 1955 it was based at various times either at Bath Road or Swindon so was on home turf when the photograph was taken. Note the locomotive is not yet carrying a shed-code plate at the base of the smoke box door, neither have rivet holes yet been inserted for a plate. The first BR Motive Power Depot coding system was introduced in 1950 so the absence of such a plate would suggest the photograph was taken prior to the application of this process to the engine. 'Reading Abbey' was finally withdrawn from Old Oak Common on 2nd July 1963, having completed a service life of over forty years. During this time it ran more than one million miles. GH439.

Image 43: At **S**windon we stop to take a look in the shed roundhouse. A fitter poses in front of a Hawksworth designed 'County 1000 Class' No. 1004 'County of Somerset'. With her fire apparently still 'in', light smoke from the chimney rises into the roof. Lurking behind her, half hidden, is **BR 'Standard Class 5MT'** 4-6-0 No. 73017, which can be identified from a similar photograph (not included), taken at the same time. In the foreground is '94xx' 0-6-0 Pannier Tank No. 9422, the number of which can just be made out from the smoke box plate. From March 1954 this was the long-term posting for 'County of Somerset' through to the end of 1960. No. 73017 was allocated to **S**windon between 1st December 1956 and 13th October 1958 when she was transferred to the Southern Region at Weymouth. Perhaps the most intriguing is No. 9422, a London Division engine which could have been in transit to or from a visit to the Works. It was based at **O**ld **O**ak Common (81A) from new in August 1950 to November 1958, then at Southall (81C) and Slough (81B) until returning to **O**ld **O**ak Common in November 1963. She was withdrawn from service there a month later. GH1456.

Image 44: George now turns his camera around and creates a very atmospheric view from inside the shed looking out into the daylight. Strewn about is the paraphernalia of a steam locomotive shed. A decrepit set of wooden steps which most certainly would not meet today's Health and Safety standards, together with a beaten-up old oil drum, occupy the foreground. Two coal shovels are also thrown indiscriminately on to the greasy cobbled floor. To the left is a hydrant, very necessary to supply water for washing out and refilling boilers. Also on the left is a 10 Ton five-plank wagon carrying the number M66838, unlikely a coal wagon as it is a bit too clean so more likely being used to carry spares or even scrap. The principal feature of the photograph is 'Castle' No. 5085 'Evesham Abbey' gleaming in ex-Works condition. 'Following 'Reading Abbey' No. 5085 was also built as a 'Star' Class engine in December 1922. In 1939 it too went back into Works and under Charles Collett was converted into a 'Castle', being out-shopped in July of that year. From October 1952 to September 1960 it was based at Bath Road (82A). During those eight years No. 5085 went back to Works five times for various forms of overhaul. Given its appearance here it is probably being run-in from the shed after repair and prior to retuning to its home shed. In the background, indistinct in the glare of the sun is a 'Hall' also facing on to the roundhouse turntable. GH434

Image 45, top: From Swindon we have run non-stop to Paddington; yet another of Brunel's iconic designs. The hands of the clock on Platform 1 stand precisely at 10.30am as a polished 'King' barks its way out of Platform 2 at the head of the 'Cornish Riviera Express'. But why was the principal train of the day not departing from Platform 1? Whatever the reason it nevertheless makes a splendid sight, glinting in the morning sunlight, as it sets out on the train's five and a half hour journey to Penzance. Obviously the 'King' will only be in charge as far as Plymouth which would make her either an Old Oak Common (81A) or Laira (83A) engine. In the summer Saturday timetable, due to pathing difficulties, this train was allowed an extra half an hour for the journey and on a Sunday a full extra hour. Meanwhile on Platform 4 stands coaching stock bearing carriage roof boards stating 'Paddington, Gloucester and Cheltenham Spa'. This could be the 10.30am arrival from Cheltenham Spa. Once cleaned and prepared it would then form the 11.15 am return service. GH141.

Image 46, opposite: It must now be just after 6.15pm and an equally important train has just arrived. An admiring passenger replete with suitcase, attaché case and mackintosh thrown over his shoulder, is persuaded to gaze up to the name board of 'The Bristolian'. The service has recently arrived on Platform 8 behind what appears to be a '70xx' series 'Castle'. Is he a friend of George's or simply someone he got into conversation with? Suffice to say all the other passengers have disappeared. Note the mailbags thrown out from the leading guards brake van, waiting on the platform for collection by postal staff. Meanwhile at Platform 7 the fireman of a less well-kept 'Hall' Class No. 4993 'Dalton Hall', a Reading (81D) engine from July 1952 to December 1959, looks back. He could be observing the stock of the train it has just brought in, being taken out by the station pilot. GH932.

Image 47: Morning interlude at Platform 2. A Guard is in conversation with the footplate crew. He could well be giving the driver the load i.e. telling him the weight of the train; information the driver requires for braking purposes. He is in charge of 'King' No.6014 'King Henry VII' which, from its appearance, has seen better days. The safety valve is blowing - a definite sin within the confines of the station - which indicates the fireman has the engine fully prepared for the road. Apart from a brief spell at Plymouth (Laira) from November 1952 to March 1954 No. 6014 was based at Stafford Road (84A) until withdrawal in September 1962. This would suggest it is heading a Birmingham (Snow Hill) and Wolverhampton train. This engine entered service in May 1928 so now would be around thirty years old and in its twilight years. Out in the sunlight beyond, a 'Castle' waits in Platform 1 at the head of what would probably be a West of England or Bristol bound express. The flight of stairs leads up to the mid-platform overbridge which affords a panoramic view of all the activity going on under Brunel's arched roof. GH933.

Image 48: The clock has moved on to just after 7 o'clock; George was often keen to record the social activity of people using the railway, and it seems railway staff, especially in their daily environment. Here he is standing on Platform 2 and sees two weary footplate men slumped on a platform seat; the fireman looks particularly spent. They have had a hard day; let's hope they are going home 'on the cushions' rather than having to work a train back. Behind the footplate men the Platform Inspector strides forward supervising the loading of the 7.10pm express to Wolverhampton (Low Level), calling at Bicester North, Banbury, Leamington Spa and Snow Hill. The train is filling up whilst others look anxiously back down the platform, possibly waiting for travelling companions to arrive. Note the lady and gentleman exchanging their fond farewells in cordial conversation at the middle door of the carriage behind the Inspector. Look also at the platform strewn with cardboard cups and rubbish. Litter is certainly not a new phenomenon. Towards the end of the decade a regular interval service left Paddington for Birmingham and Wolverhampton hourly at ten minutes past the hour between 9.10am and 8.10pm. **GH931.**

Image 49: Now the clock has moved on yet again to just after 8 o'clock; darkness has fallen and in contrast to the previous photograph this picture could well be entitled, 'parting is such sweet sorrow'. A lady stands in the carriage doorway, her arm draped around the gentleman's neck. With his left hand in his coat pocket he looks rather forlorn. Are they looking back for the Guard's green flag, hoping it will never appear? For well over a century the railway station had always been the point of parting between family, friends and loved ones; never so dramatic as during the course of two World Wars. The train? Well the most likely contender as it is standing in Platform 2 would be the 8.5pm to Bath and Bristol, the last midweek train of the day. The clue is in the coach roof board. It also appears to be well loaded with all the compartments in view occupied. Perhaps George saw the poignancy of the situation and took this photograph on instinct. GH924.

PADDINGTON   NEWPORT   AN

Image 50, above: Now the station is almost deserted except for a solitary lady passenger seated on a bench on Platform 1. Brunel's symmetrical arch spanning Platforms 1 and 2 is gracefully enhanced above the bright lighting. It is almost a ghostly scene; Paddington is almost asleep. The time on the station clock indicates it to be approaching 7.40. We may assume this is an autumn or winter early evening view and clearly we are in the mid-1950s. The train in Platform 2 has recently arrived and its few passengers have decamped, either to taxis, buses or the tube; its locomotive trapped at the end buffer stops. The van in the foreground is 'Siphon G' - the GWR Telegraphic code' for a milk wagon. The 'Siphon G' was the ultimate development of earlier designs to carry unprocessed milk, in churns, direct from the farm to milk processing plants at the point of delivery. One hundred and thirty of these bogie vehicles were produced between 1913 and 1927. All survived into BR ownership, the first being withdrawn in 1954, the last in 1962. GH920.

Image 51, left: Clearly George found Paddington a very atmospheric and emotive place to be and it brought to the fore his skill in taking night-time photographs in this further example. The lights on Platform 1 shine on the station clock whose fingers are now approaching 9.30pm. With the night closing in and the lights on in the carriage sitting in the platform, directly beneath the clock, it may well be the passenger's homeward journey. Standing in Platform 2 and fully loaded, this train could be a slightly delayed 9.25pm to Cardiff, again a last such train of the day, which called at Swindon at 11.23pm. So let us use a little licence and travel with this service back to Swindon…. GH917.

Image 52: No stop at Swindon would be complete without a visit to the Works where George managed to record something quite unique. Narrow-gauge 'Vale of Rheidol' 2-6-2 Tank No. 9 in for overhaul. At that time, of course, the Vale of Rheidol was still run and owned by British Railways. No.9 had two sister engines, No.7 'Owain Glyndwr' and No.8 'Llewellyn'. These two were built together in 1923 at Swindon to replace previous engines. Meanwhile, No.9 was erected using some of the parts of previous 'V of R' locomotives and returned to Aberystwyth as virtually a new engine in 1932. In 1955/6 No.9 was returned to Swindon for overhaul at which time she was given the name 'Prince of Wales'. Note the rivet holes have not yet been applied to the side of the tank for the name board to be affixed. Some wag in the erecting shop has chalked onto the smoke box door, 'Frying tonight'. GH1471.

Image 53: Freshly out-shopped after overhaul and highly polished, looking absolutely magnificent and ready for the road; a portrait of '4073 Castle' No 7000 'Viscount Portal'. This locomotive was built at Swindon and released into service in May 1946. Her first allocation was Newton Abbot (83A) and on her smoke box door it can be seen that in the 1950s, this was still her allocation. The engine was named in honour of the part Charles Portal, Marshal of the Royal Air Force, 1st Viscount Portal of Hungerford, in recognition of the part he played during the Second World War. Between 1950 and 1960 the engine went to Swindon no less than eight times for attention; on six occasions her boiler was changed whilst five of the visits were for a heavy general overhaul. She appears to have been photographed in front of the Carriage Workshops given the rakes of coaches behind her. On the left, the most prominent of these is one with a bow-ended roof; the distinctive profile of a Frederick Hawksworth designed corridor coach. GH1455.

Image 54, top: From Swindon we now head towards Gloucester a route that takes us down the Gloucestershire Golden Valley. Due to its scenic setting it is appropriately named and being within cycling distance of George's home in the north of Bristol, was one of his favourite haunts. Consequently it became the location of many of his most memorable photographs and this is a Heiron classic. From a vantage point high above the mouth of Sapperton tunnel at the head of the valley, George has captured the 'Cheltenham Spa Express' clambering its way up the last hundred yards into the tunnel mouth. It carries the Reporting No. 'A09'. This is a post 1960 photograph after reporting numbers had been overhauled and the letter represented the destination district, in this case Paddington. In moments the single-chimney 'Castle' and its train will disappear into the cavern, with exhaust strokes beating off the tunnel walls in a crescendo as the train approaches the summit of the climb. The 'Cheltenham Spa Express' left Cheltenham Spa (St. James) at 8am calling at Malvern Road and Gloucester Central (for reversal) where the 'Castle' would have taken control of the train. It then called at Stonehouse, Stroud and Kemble before running fast to Paddington where it was due at 10.35am. GH1246.

Image 55, right: From a similar position; a wonderfully panoramic view taken in 1957, a train slowly snaking its way towards Sapperton Tunnel. Despite being only yards from the tunnel mouth it still has over a mile to go before it reaches the summit and the fireman will be able to take a well earned rest from his back breaking work. In such circumstances the footplate crew had to work in harmony if the fire was to produce enough steam for the engine's requirements. It would not be uncommon for the driver to take over the shovel from the fireman to enable him to take a breather. It is clearly a hot summer day as the exhaust from the chimney of 'Modified Hall' No. 7903 'Foremarke Hall', throughout the decade an Old Oak Common (81A) engine, is almost clear vapour before it turns to white steam. The 'Down' distance signal adjacent to the first coach on the 'Up' side of the tracks is that for Frampton Crossing. It was placed here to give the footplate men on trains emerging from the tunnel the best possible sighting. Note also the platelayers hut in the foreground. In front of it is a grinding wheel sitting in its cradle; an invaluable piece of equipment for the men to sharpen a sickle and scythe. Not only did the permanent way gang look after the track but they also controlled the vegetation on the lineside. This undergrowth was occasionally deliberately set on fire in order to check its spread. This was known as 'setting fire to the batter' as the embankment was known. The lengthsman was responsible for controlling such a fire so that it did not encroach on neighbouring farmland. GH1280.

Image 56: Further down the valley and approaching the tunnel, a superb rail level view of a highly polished 'Castle', No. 5018 'St. Mawes Castle' with its boiler glinting in the sunlight. Her appearance is an absolute credit to the Gloucester cleaners whose code she carries and which was her home shed from February 1951 to April 1958, apart from short intervening spells at Worcester and Cardiff (Canton). She is in fine fettle, her pure white steam exhaust standing against the backcloth of a clear blue summer sky. Oozing power she gallops through the Gloucestershire countryside taking the rising gradient in her stride. For the first 80 yards into the tunnel the 1 in 65 gradient stiffens to 1 in 57 thereafter easing to 1 in 90 throughout the remaining length. Heading Train '730', she is raising the echoes of the wooded upper stretches of the valley as she passes. From 1953 to 1958 this train was a permanent fixture in the summer timetable as the 11.45am (SO) Cheltenham Spa to Paddington. GH1244. (See also image No. 62.)

Image 57: In the opposite direction, a very well kept 'Hall' No. 6917 'Oldlands Hall' emerges from the western end of Sapperton Tunnel into the daylight in charge of a stopping train bound for Gloucester. During the second half of the decade this was a Gloucester (85B) based engine so was working her way home. The odd looking post on the right with a circular face backed by a hood was a 40mph permanent speed restriction sign for the descent to Chalford. The somewhat dilapidated sign board alongside the 'Up' line reads "Whistle frequently when passing through the tunnel". It probably had more relevance when the ganger would be checking his length to ensure all the rail chair keys were in place and securely holding the rails tight. The western tunnel is actually one of a pair and at 1 mile and 104 yards in length is by far the longer of the two. The summit of the line is in the short gap between the two. Brunel redesigned the tunnel to make it shallower so as to avoid a layer of Fuller's Earth, which was not sufficiently stable to allow the construction of a tunnel. This led to a steeper gradient towards the mouth of the tunnel which then eased to 1 in 90 in the main tunnel. GH1250.

Image 58: The Swindon - Gloucester line was equally as important for freight traffic as it was for passengers as and was the alternative route to South Wales from London and the south-east; keeping slow moving trains off the direct (via Badminton and the Severn Tunnel) London to South Wales main line. In this case Hall' class No. 4999 'Gopsal Hall' has also just emerged from Sapperton Tunnel at the head of an Class 'F' express freight consisting of a long rake of empty coal wagons, this being an unfitted train. It would have previously stopped at the top of the incline to have the brakes on some of the wagons pinned down before making the cautious descent at 1 in 60, at this point, through the valley to Brimscombe. The train would be heading back to the South Wales coalfield for another load. Although the 'Halls' were notionally a Class 5 mixed traffic No. 4999 appears to have spent most of the decade based primarily at freight sheds such as St. Phillips Marsh (82B) and Cardiff (Canton) (86C) with only a brief period for summer passenger traffic at Bath Road (82A) in 1956, hence perhaps, her somewhat unkempt appearance. GH74.

Image 59: Meanwhile in the 'Up' direction another engine hard at work in the upper reaches of the Golden Valley is approaching Sapperton Tunnel but this time it is a workaday freight locomotive battling against the gradient with its train of steel girders and coal. The contrast in her appearance compared to a passenger train could not be more marked. This '28xx' class 2-8-0 No. 3826 was quite used to the grime of coal and steel, she spent most of her career in South Wales at Pontypool Road (86G) hauling trains such as this. These locomotives were known as being of the 'Heavy Freight' type and were designed specifically for this type of work. It does not appear to have any banking assistance at the rear of the train, but of course the train may be longer than we can see. The headlamp code (Class H) indicates that it is a through freight not fitted with the automatic brake therefore slow moving. This explains why the train is on Sapperton Bank; it has been routed away from the Severn Tunnel and the main line; instead being sent from Severn Tunnel Junction via Gloucester in order to reach Swindon and beyond. GH1197.

Image 60: A little further down the valley a 'Castle' No. 7006 'Lydford Castle' heads home to Gloucester, where she was based, with a ten coach express. No. 7006 was at Gloucester (85B) from August 1948 to February 1958 apart from a short interlude at Swindon (82C) in 1950/51. The train has just glided past the Chalford 'Down' distance signal descending the gradient on what has now become 1 in 74. Hence steam is shut off and the brakes are probably lightly applied to keep the speed of the train in check. A notice board can be seen on the 'Up' side of the line. This reads 'Catch Point 400 yards'. Catch Points are a railway safety device and were placed here because of the steepness of the gradient. Should a coupling snap between wagons on a loose-coupled freight, any wagons rolling backwards would automatically become derailed instead of running backwards down the bank and potentially into another train; as had happened at Armagh, Northern Ireland in June 1889 with disastrous results. **GH120.**

Image 61: Storming Sapperton. '4073 Castle' No. 5041 'Tiverton Castle', a Neath (Court Sart) (87A) based engine according to her shed plate code, is having to work hard as she passes Milepost 97. Now was there ever a locomotive with a more chequered career? Each shed she was posted to during the decade subsequently put her into store. However, in June 1961 she went to Neath and operated out of there until April 1962 when she was again returned to store. This picture was therefore probably taken between these dates. Milepost 97 would place the Gloucester-Paddington express about a mile up the valley from Chalford. It shows the steepness of its southern shoulders; the line being built on a ledge cut into the valley side. This bridge known locally as Jackdaw Bridge had its own incline of 1 in 2.9 giving access from a farm on the hillside to fields in the valley below. The locomotive is passing over an ATC ramp - the contact shoe on the engine can just be seen - which must be for the Frampton 'Up' Distance Signal. The GWR was in the forefront of cab signalling, introducing its Automatic Train Control as early as 1906. Its purpose was twofold; first to display the aspect of the distant signal in the cab with an audible warning to the driver and second to bring the train to a stand if the warning was ignored. It was particularly useful in fog or falling snow. With only slight modifications it was a system that lasted well into the BR days until eventually superseded by the (non-contact) standard British Railways Automatic Warning System (AWS). GH1266.

Image 62: Another view of the train we saw earlier (Image No. 56) and quite possibly the same engine. Almost the perfect picture and one that encapsulates the captivating thrill of witnessing a steam engine in all its glory. Sapperton Bank with its final gradient of 1 in 60 to the summit was one of those ultimate stretches that tested a locomotive to its limits. Sapping the strength of the fireman to create sufficient steam, both man and machine would have to work flat out to enable the train to keep to time. It is little wonder the Golden Valley kept drawing George back to record the final chapter of the steam story. With Train Reporting Number '730' an immaculately presented '50xx' series 'Castle' raises the echoes as she storms her way up the valley from Chalford, pouring clouds of steam from its clean chimney, She is approaching Marley Lane Bridge just east of Chalford, part of the village able to be glimpsed in the background. GH1193.

Image 63: The echoes reverberate around the Cotswold stone village of Chalford as '43xx' 2-6-0 No. 6370 battles its way up the Golden Valley. With the gradient against it the going is getting increasingly tough as the valley begins to close in; it is tackling it without the aid of a Brimscombe banker. The train is a Class 'H' unfitted through freight of sheeted wagons that are most probably general goods. The '43xx' type were designed by George Jackson Churchward and introduced from 1911 onwards. This particular locomotive was out-shopped from Swindon in April 1921 and was one of a total of 217 such engines built. It spent most of the decade in South Wales. For six years, between October 1954 and September 1960 at Ebbw Junction (86A) before moving on to Pontypool Road, so there is little doubt where the train originated. **GH144.**

Image 64, above: High summer in Gloucestershire and George has again captured an evocative scene; three young ladies dressed in the summer attire redolent of the early 1950s watch the Chalford auto train ascend the valley. This scene was recorded near St. Mary's Crossing Halt on an August afternoon in 1953. The train is hauled by a diminutive '14xx Class' 0-4-2T No. 1424. Designed by Charles Collett; it was released into service from Swindon Works in November 1933 and originally given the number 4824. It was renumbered to 1424 in 1948. These little engines always looked to be a far older design with their quaint but nevertheless endearing appearance, although they could be surprisingly sprightly. Their looks did not prevent a number of them from performing sterling work over many years on the Gloucester to Chalford push-pull service and it was also known on occasions to unofficially race alongside an express out from Gloucester as far as Standish Junction. No. 1424 was based at Gloucester for fourteen years from December 1949 to November 1963, when condemned and scrapped six months later at Cashmore's, Great Bridge, Birmingham. GH unlisted.

Image 65, opposite: Evening on Sapperton Bank. Against the backdrop of a threatening sky, 'Hall' No. 5980 'Dingley Hall', emerges from beneath Marley Lane overbridge above Chalford. From March 1962 until she was withdrawn in September 1962 she was based at Gloucester (85B) and is here tackling the final assault to the summit. Although hauling only five coaches, Sapperton is taking its toll as the exhaust blasts into the sky against the darkening clouds. The lengthening shadows indicate the sun is sinking in the west. A Class 'B' head code tells us it is a stopping train. A glance at the Western Region timetable of the period shows that there was a 6.33pm stopping train from Cheltenham Spa which left Gloucester for Swindon at 7pm. Its last call was at Chalford at 7.36pm. Assuming this to be the service, the engine has just had to resume the journey on the 1 in 60 climb from a standing start. The result is captured in this picture. The sound of the exhaust can be imagined as No. 5980 thunders her way past the camera. GH1179.

Image 66: Following on with a change of season we have a very atmospheric view taken on a misty-moisty morning. A beautifully constructed photograph putting together the natural surroundings of the area and the railway environment to make the complete picture. The footpath in the foreground leads the eye into this view. The late autumn/winter morning adds to the atmosphere as Gloucester (Horton Road) (85B) based '14xx Class' 0-4-2T No. 1406 hustles the Chalford auto-train somewhere up the lower reaches of the Golden Valley between Stroud and its destination. The Gloucester to Chalford auto trains were the last to survive on the Western Region. The Working Timetable described the train as a 'Rail-Motor', itself a throwback to much earlier times when steam railmotors were the norm. In this operation seen here, the footplate crew worked the train as normal from the footplate on the outward journey whilst on the return the Driver operated the regulator from the front of the coach connected by a bar under the floor of the auto coach back to the engine. He could also control the brake from a conventional valve. Meanwhile the Fireman remained on the footplate to keep up the steam supply, adjust the steam cut-off (the reverser) and maintain the engine. The last service ran on the 31ˢᵗ October 1964. A more atmospheric portrait would be difficult to find. **GH1408.**

Image 67: St. Mary's Crossing was deep in the Golden Valley, between Brimscombe and Chalford. In signalling terms it was simply a non-block post on the climb to Sapperton. Brimscombe was at the bottom of the ruling 1 in 65 climb and the home of a small sub-shed of Gloucester (85B). Here we see an ex-Great Western 'Large Prairie' '51xx' Class 2-6-2T banking a freight train up the incline past St. Mary's Crossing Signal Box. Ten of these locomotives were allocated to Gloucester (85B) during the latter part of the decade with a number being out stationed at Brimscombe specifically for this purpose. Not only was St. Mary's Crossing the site of a minor level crossing, which connected a minor road from the small hamlet of Hyde to the main A419 trunk road which ran through the valley; but of a small wooden 'Halt' served by the auto-trains which ran between Gloucester and Chalford . Part of the train's load is a consignment of Field Artillery Guns; the military still being large users of the railway fifteen years after hostilities had ceased at the end of the Second World War. GH1248.

Image 68: Now we arrive at Gloucester Central; the Great Western station in the city. A sprightly looking Porter with his barrow, in customary pose (hands in pockets), watches something ahead whilst a passenger service stands on the 'Up' side platform. The crew of the unidentified 'Castle' Class engine are similarly both intently looking out from the offside of the locomotive but no doubt also with an eye on the elevated 'ground signal' which when cleared to 'off' would also be their 'right away'. (The platforms at Gloucester were long enough for two trains to use the same platform hence the signals and crossovers mid-way.) The platform clock tells us that it has just gone 7 o'clock. Their anxious looks may feasibly account for this train being the 6.33pm ex Cheltenham Spa, which having reversed direction here, with the 'Castle' now backed on to the train, it forms the 7pm departure; semi-fast to Swindon due there at 8.20pm. Meanwhile a tank engine running bunker first enters the 'Down' platform. Its headlamp code is not fully discernible but from the lamp in the middle of the top of the bunker it may well be an ordinary passenger or branch passenger working, either being likely given the waiting passengers. **GH1.**

Image 69: This time from the same platform we are looking west at Gloucester Central towards Over Junction. The arriving train hauled by what appears to be a Mogul has just disgorged a squad of lads in army uniform. Appearing to be quite young it is likely that they are part of the Combined Cadet Force which many schools in the 50s participated in. The CCF was formed in 1948. It was, and still is, an educational partnership between schools and the Ministry of Defence. Summer Camps are a regular feature of their activities. The platform clock tells us that it is 2.20pm and from the anxious expressions on their faces it could well be that the lads may be on their outward journey rather than going back home! They could be in the course of changing trains here as they are heading in the direction of the long footbridge which connected Central with Eastgate (Midland) station. Given the length of the train it could be the 12.25pm Birmingham (Snow Hill) to Carmarthen running about half an hour late. Opposite there is another recent arrival, the ex GWR Railcar pulled up behind an 'Up' train in the opposite platform, likely to have arrived via what is now the long closed branch from Ledbury. This therefore pre-dates the photograph as before 13th July 1959 when the branch from Ledbury to Gloucester closed to passenger traffic. GH2.

Image 70: We now head south taking the route of the old Bristol and Gloucester Railway to arrive at Standish Junction where the Great Western line diverged from the Midland route to Bristol to head up the Golden Valley. A resplendent 'Castle' No. 5018 'St. Mawes Castle' gets the road for Swindon. She approaches the junction with a light 'Up' express made up of eight coaches. The track work from Gloucester to this point was quadrupled, essentially each route having its own independent 'Up' and 'Down' lines, as the signals indicate. Throughout much of the 1950s 'St. Mawes Castle' was the pride of Horton Road Shed and kept in pristine condition. But the daily toil of the haul up Sapperton Bank took its toll on her. Happily her full service record survives. Between November 1951 and January 1959 she went back to Swindon Works for attention five times. This included three Heavy Intermediate and two Heavy General overhauls. One of the latter from 3rd January 1957 lasted 128 days. The curtain came down on her career when she was withdrawn from Reading (81D) in March 1964. She had completed around 1.5 million miles. **GH1284.**

Image 71: Following the old Bristol and Gloucester we eventually come to Charfield. This allows us to witness a typical and magical Heiron photograph. Here George constructs a composition using his wife Shirley and son Richard to bring warmth and a connection to his picture; this time using as the scene an evening family outing, possibly a picnic. An unidentified 'Hall' Class locomotive heads a Bristol bound Class 'C' freight (fitted throughout with the automatic vacuum brake operative on not less than half of the vehicles piped to the engine). It is comprised mainly of vans heading south through the Gloucestershire landscape near Charfield with Wotton-under-Edge and the Cotswold Hills beyond. The contrast between light and shade is captured perfectly; the impression given is one of a perfect outing in the countryside, if one is a railway enthusiast of course! The hay has been baled in the field beyond the tracks so autumn cannot be far away. GH635.

Image 72: Moving further south on the same main line we get a wonderfully artistic view of a train framed in the shallow arch of a substantially constructed minor road overbridge. The setting is Rangeworthy just south of Wickwar. A '4900 Hall' Class No. 5992 'Horton Hall' heads south with a Class 'C' train of 'perishables' made up of a mixture of four wheeled vehicles. Would they be carrying fruit and vegetables from the Vale of Evesham or perhaps further afield? Throughout the 1950s and early 1960's No. 5992 was based at West-Country depots. It spent the first six months of 1965 based at Gloucester, although in this shot she is bereft of a shed code plate. Alas in July she was transferred to Ebbw Junction at Newport, formerly (86A), which by September 1963, had been redesignated as (86B). From here she was withdrawn from service and condemned. In this picture she does look rather time worn but operationally in good order. However, in 1965 the Western Region was determined to rid itself of all its steam engines so perhaps her demise was rather premature. From the appearance of the sky and the length of the shadows we may deduce that it is, once again, a summer evening. Just in front of Wickwar tunnel mouth an aqueduct spans the tracks surmounted by a public footpath. A couple on this bridge take time out to watch the train go by. **GH662.**

Image 73, above: A view south of Yate on the Westerleigh north to west curve, taken from a point just south of Westerleigh North Junction Signal Box. The train is a heavy freight, undoubtedly loose-coupled and headed by a BR Standard Class '9F' 2-10-0 locomotive. It is hauling at least 46 wagons and the brake van hasn't yet come into view. Of those 36 are coal wagons of various types with some loaded and others empty, nine vans and a bogie bolster wagon loaded with steel beams make up the train. Approaching Westerleigh West Junction and the Western main line from Paddington to Filton Junction and South Wales the train is very likely bound for Stoke Gifford Yard for resorting. The 2-10-0's were the final class built by British Railways. Undoubtedly very capable engines and equally at home on a passenger train over the Mendips on the Somerset and Dorset line, as they were on a heavy train like this. **GH1261.**

Image 74, opposite: For continuity we have now headed back east from Westerleigh Junction along the South Wales main line towards Swindon to pick up our journey west. A Cardiff (Canton) (86C) 'Britannia' No, 70025 'Western Star' races through Hullavington halfway along the 1 in 300 climb from Little Somerford to Badminton with the 'Down' 'Capitals United Express'. She has had a good run at it on the preceding seven miles descent from Wootton Basset and looks to be making headway for an on time arrival at Badminton. This train was inaugurated on Monday 6th February 1956 running between Swansea and Paddington and return. In the summer of the same year the 'Down' train was given the Reporting Number '171' leaving Paddington, as always, at 3.55pm. It ran on every weekday and conveyed through coaches to Neyland, the Restaurant Car being taken off at Swansea. The only call between Paddington and Newport was the feudal stop at Badminton at 5.44pm. **GH82.**

Image 75: Moving west, it is English high summer at Alderton, and the dandelion clocks blowing in the gentle breeze tell us it is just after eleven o'clock as the 'Up' 'Red Dragon' races between Badminton and Hullavington. In charge is 'Britannia' No. 70025 'Western Star', a Canton locomotive, showing little exhaust on the falling gradient. This was another of George's favoured locations. A contrasting photograph taken from much the same position, but also featuring the same engine appears on page 39 of his book, 'Roaming the Western Rails' (1980). In that picture she is seen forging through snow on 30th January 1954. Did George do this deliberately to portray the different seasons? It is certainly mere coincidence that it is the same locomotive but reasonable to suppose that both pictures were taken during the same period of the decade. GH147.

Image 76: Badminton was, for George, the place to be above all others. Its quintessential atmosphere as a beautifully maintained rural railway station perhaps set it aside above other locations. A '4073' 'Castle' Class 4-6-0, very probably No. 5072 'Hurricane', runs through the station on the 'Down' main line; from her exhaust it would appear accelerating from a signal or permanent-way check. She is in charge of a train displaying Reporting No. '163'. In the summer of 1952 this was introduced as an additional working, on Monday to Friday, as the 08.55am Paddington to Pembroke Dock. It became very popular and from 1955 to 1956 ran through the winter as well. During the summer of 1958 it continued to run every weekday. Between 1947 and January 1957 'Hurricane' was a South Wales based engine allocated during that period to both Landore and Canton. From the appearance of the flower beds in the foreground which are still in their winter state together with the trees in the background with only early foliage, it has all the hallmarks of an early springtime view. If this is the case the photograph would appear to have been taken in early 1956 when local services were still calling at the station, hence what appears to be a milk churn on the 'down' platform awaiting collection. **GH41.**

Image 77: One of the reasons which attracted George to Badminton was that some of the fast express workings between Paddington and South Wales, and vice versa, were obliged to call there. It is almost eight o'clock on a pleasant summer evening and the shadows are lengthening as 'Castle' No. 5080 'Defiant', rolls into the station with the heavy 'Down' 'Red Dragon'. This seemingly insignificant wayside station is the second call for this train on its journey from Paddington to South Wales. The reason for its stop can be traced back to the development of the South Wales Direct Railway which opened in 1903, obviating the need for trains to South Wales having to run via Bristol. From the outset the GWR entered into a written agreement with the Duke of Beaufort undertaking that four passenger trains would call at the station every day and additionally any train should stop there if required to do so by a First Class ticket holder. Over time this developed into two express trains each way being booked to stop at Badminton, one of which being the train pictured here. GH406.

Image 78: In complete seasonal contrast to the previous photograph and emphasising the point that George took his photographs in all kinds of conditions we now find ourselves at the same location, except this time it is winter and in an inhospitable landscape we are looking at 'Britannia' No.70029 'Shooting Star' drawing out of Badminton with the 'Down' 'Red Dragon'. It is obviously very cold and George has had extreme patience to get the shot he wanted. It shows his tenacity and as he explained in 'Trains to the West' on another winter evening when the snow was much deeper he caused some alarm! '*One night I stood there in the snow for nearly an hour – the train was late as a result of some frozen points somewhere on the way from Paddington. I was standing in snow up to my knees. Before long the stationmaster, escorted by a porter carrying a hand-lamp, trudged through the snow off the end of Badminton Station platform and approached me: "What are you doing?" said the stationmaster. "Freezing!" I replied. "You must want your head reading!" was his retort.* But after one of George's shots was subsequently published in 'Trains Illustrated', from then on he was provided with tea in the stationmaster's house. GH887.

Image 79: Another definite skill was his development of night-time photography. An absolute Heiron Classic; one that you may say could not be improved upon. George became the past master of this genre. He would take himself out at all hours, in all seasons and as we know all types of weather in order to obtain the ultimate photograph and arguably this is one of them. With steam to spare and whistle chiming 'Britannia' No. 70022 'Tornado' sets forth from Badminton with the 'Down' 'Capitals United Express'. George was a pioneer with his first experiments in 1953. In his book, 'Portraits of Steam', published by **OPC** in 2000, George explains how he took his photographs at Badminton. '*I used a big open flash gun with a long reflector- much more effective than a domestic light bulb and it was a case of one bulb, one flash. Usually I mounted the camera on a tripod and having opened the lens, left it open for as long as possible, sometimes as much as eight minutes. I then walked to a spot side-on to the engine to flash the gun'.* I think we can agree; the result is magical. Possibly George used this photograph as the basis for the artwork which adorned the sleeve of his book 'Trains to the West' but this time featuring No. 70028 'Royal Star'. Perhaps the change came about as a result of a commission? Certainly the Ian Allan company which firm had published 'Trains to the West' sported several Heiron original paintings on the office walls. GH882.

Image 80, opposite: Another nocturne shot, possibly taken on a winter evening, this time featuring 'Britannia' Class No. 70029 'Shooting Star'. With clear exhaust from the chimney, safety valves blowing and express code lamps glowing like cats eyes caught in headlights, it swings into motion taking its leave from Badminton with the down 'Red Dragon'. Given the long exposure time, even the Mark 1 coaches glow with their modern compartment lighting and George gets that exposure absolutely right. In many senses, the fact that express trains called at Badminton served George's experiments with night-time photography very well. No. 70029 went to Canton from new in November 1952 and remained until September 1961 when it went north to Aston (then 21D). Intriguingly, according to **SLS** records, from May to July 1953 No. 70029 was tested on the Southern Region working out of Exmouth Junction shed (72A) but was quite quickly returned to Canton. It has been suggested that the 'Britannias' numbered between 70015 and 70029, excepting No. 70018 'Flying Dutchman', were deliberately named after **GWR** broad gauge locomotives as they were intended for the Western Region. GH884.

Image 81, below: Back in the daylight; a study of a footplate crew whose train has been 'put into the loop'. The scene is still Badminton on the 'Down' side. Their locomotive, an ex-GW 2-6-0, stands at the platform starting signal. They seem to be in deep discussion about some subject or another to the point that they are totally oblivious to the westbound 'Pembroke Coast Express' speeding past. No coal needs bringing forward from the tender; the engine doesn't require any attention. There is nothing to do but wait. This was the experience of many a goods train crew in the days of steam. It was worse for the Guard in his van at the back of the train; he had nobody to talk to! GH857.

Image 82: Now a late summer morning at Badminton and the sun shines. Suddenly the calm is shattered as the 'Up' 'Red Dragon' breezes effortlessly through. This thirteen coach train is headed by a Cardiff (Canton) (86C) 'Britannia' 4-6-2 No. 70027 'Rising Star'. After she arrives at Paddington at 1pm she would have gone to Ranelagh Bridge Depot just outside the station to be serviced and turned. Taking up the return 'Down' working, which left Paddington at 5.55pm, extraordinarily, that train would make its second stop at this quiet wayside station. The reason for this was a development of the agreement signed in 1899 between the GWR and the Duke of Beaufort part of which decreed that any train had to stop at Badminton if a first class passenger wished to alight. GH879.

Image 83: An 'Up' local pulls out of Badminton headed by 'Castle' Class No. 5048 'Earl of Devon'; the Driver looking quizzically towards the camera. This locomotive was one of the 21 'Earls' intended for naming in the 'Dukedog' Class. (See image 93*). However, the extra interest in this photograph is the horse box, lurking in the siding just beyond the platform, behind the locomotive. Since the birth of the railway era, horse traffic had been a quintessential part of railway transport both to races and other equine events until the development of mechanised road transport. Horses are synonymous with Badminton. In former years the **GWR** carried enormous amounts of people and horses too, to follow the Beaufort Hunt. In May of each year since 1949 Badminton has hosted an equine three-day event. Not only does that tell us when the picture was likely to have been taken but it also implies that horses attending were still being carried by rail well into the 1950s. **GH674.**

Image 84, left: Now back to the nocturne and a captivatingly atmospheric view, taken on an autumn/winter evening, of 'Britannia' Class No. 70016 'Ariel', by 1959 a Canton (86C) based engine. George had a predilection for 'Britannias'; they were, bar a few 9Fs, the principal BR Standard Class he photographed. He had also become the leading exponent of his generation in night-time railway photography. In this picture reminiscent in some ways of the style of the great O Winston-Link he has produced the perfect exposure. He had developed his own method of achieving this (see image 80) using a tripod, one of the few times he ever used one, and a separate independent flashbulb. Here the result is magnificent and the footplate man looks pleased to be involved. The setting is the eastern end of Badminton Station and with an abundance of steam in the twilight. The only train with a scheduled stop at Badminton at about this time during the late 1950's and early 1960s, was the 12.5pm Neyland/Milford Haven to Paddington, due away around 5.12pm. GH672.

Image 85, opposite top: We now continue our journey west to witness a train having just emerged from Sodbury tunnel. It is English high summer and the photographer, as his point of perspective, uses the bush blooming in the foreground. Here we are on the curve of the shallow cutting approaching Badminton. In the background the first bridge seen is the aqueduct carrying a small stream across the cutting near the eastern mouth of Sodbury tunnel from which smoke is still emerging. An immaculate 'Castle' No. 7012 'Barry Castle', with steam shut off, breasts the summit of the long climb from Winterbourne and prepares for the descent to Somerford, heading her eleven coach 'Up' express from South Wales to Paddington. During the decade 'Barry Castle' spent nine years of her career based at Landore (87E), from 1950 to 1959, and the carriage roof boards support the evidence that this may be a West Wales to Paddington express. GH118.

Image 86, opposite bottom: The eastern end of the two mile Sodbury tunnel where a 'Hymek' speeds out into the limelight and enters a very lunar landscape. George is in the 'four-foot' to get his desired shot but it is hard to believe we are in the midst of South Gloucestershire countryside. On the right is an unusual platelayers hut built into the steep sided cutting. The 'Hymeks' were unique in that they were not part of the 1955 modernisation plan but were developed for the Western Region which opted for lightweight locomotives with hydraulic transmission when funds were allocated by the BTC. They were the only Type 3 diesel hydraulic locomotives to be built. 101 machines were delivered with their colloquial name derived from their Hydraulic Mekydro transmission. They became Class 35, and the first was introduced in 1961. Originally all were allocated to Bath Road, Canton and Old Oak Common depots. This particular Hymek is displaying Headcode '1A35'. In June 1962 former train reporting numbers and headlamp codes were combined into one train reporting number, '1A35' being the code for the 'Up' 'Red Dragon' express from South Wales to Paddington. GH870.

Image 87: At the other end of the tunnel we see an express heading for Wales. For the bulk of the decade from 1952 to 1957 the train carrying the reporting number '170' referred to the summer weekday 3.45pm Paddington to Fishguard Harbour. With re-organisation in 1958 this changed to the 12.55pm (SO) Paddington to Swansea. Bearing this code an unidentified 'Castle' Class 4-6-0 emerges from the west end of Sodbury Tunnel passing milepost 133¾ from Paddington. With a wisp of smoke from its chimney the locomotive is running freely down the 1 in 300 gradient from the summit at Badminton. Its tender is raising the dust indicating that the scoop is lowered ready to take up water from the troughs the train is about to run on to. The atmosphere, with fluffy cotton bud cumulus clouds in the summer sky, is almost palpable. All the elements work together to make a perfect scene for the photographer. **GH992.**

Image 88: A reprise of a Heiron classic at Sodbury water troughs but a brilliant photograph.
A splendidly presented Canton based 'Castle' heads the westbound 'Capitals United Express'. Under a warm summer sky the photographer is about to get drenched but the result was worth it. Water troughs were positioned in strategic places. Sodbury was one of only two on the GW main line between Paddington and the Severn Tunnel, the other being at Basildon between Pangbourne and Goring. They were essential for non-stop expresses. Sodbury troughs, 1,570 feet in length, were set on a short 620 yards level stretch of track at the western end of the tunnel. In the midst of the twelve miles of 1 in 300 falling gradient from Badminton to Winterbourne, the water supply was obtained from the infant River Frome being carried over the railway by the aqueduct at the back of the train. GH975.

Image 89: And here is the original absolute classic; well worthy of inclusion here. Running on to Sodbury water troughs in 1961, Britannia Class No. 70024 'Vulcan' heads the westbound 'Capitals United Express'. GH948.

Image 90: A picture marking the transition from steam to diesel. From the end of the 'Down' platform at Chipping Sodbury a photograph which is beautifully balanced between the signal box on the right and the goods yard on the left. The train, headed by a pair of North British Type 2 Diesel Hydraulics of the 'D6300' series, working in tandem, is heading west. This class of diesel was introduced in 1959 and with the chalk markings on the buffers and the number of men visible in the cab of the leading locomotive this could well be a trial run out from Swindon; a point emphasised by the melange of carriages in tow. The very first of this class of diesels were allocated to Plymouth (Laira) (83A) and the next batch followed on to Old Oak Common. Note that there is still plenty of work in the yard. Also the cast iron sign attached to the signal box wall politely advising passengers to make use of the footbridge rather than the skewed barrow crossing at the platform end. **GH969.**

Image 91: At the other end of the station 'Castle' No. 7003 'Elmley Castle' is on the four and a half mile, 1 in 300 descent, from Sodbury Tunnel to Winterbourne as it breezes through at the head of 'The Pembroke Coast Express'. In 1955 she was a Landore (87E) allocated engine. This train left Paddington at 10.55am and on weekdays was due to arrive at Newport at 1.6pm, so the time must have been around 12.30pm. The train in the 'Down' platform is the 11.44am Swindon to Bristol stopping train in charge of Hawksworth 'County' Class No. 1005 'County of Devon', a Bath Road (82A) engine at the time. There does not appear to be too much activity on the stopper but at least one carriage door is open. A period touch is added by what appears to be a Dad, quite possibly a railwayman himself, engaging the train crew in conversation. Has he brought his young son down to the station to watch the trains go by? The picture was taken on 31st March, 1955. GH988.

Image 92: Fresh fruit and vegetables from London or are they empties returning to South Wales and the West Country for another consignment? Another portrayal of life generally, during the 1950s decade. Again the scene is Chipping Sodbury. 'Castle' No. 5084 'Reading Abbey' pounds through the station with a Class 'C' train of perishables. The fascinating fact is that this is a 'Down' train and from the shadow cast by the 'Up' side station canopy, it is evening. A more aesthetic scene would be hard to find; the peace and tranquillity of a country station being shattered by the passage of a train. On the platform the spectacle is viewed by another father and son. The little boy has his night-time snuggles with him; one of them possibly being a home produced knitted rabbit. Beyond, arms folded, is an older gentleman replete in trilby hat, jacket and baggy trousers matched with hob-nailed boots. Are they prospective passengers or have they also just come out to watch the trains go by? If the latter, what a wonderful way to spend an evening. GH436.

Image 93: An old stalwart on Permanent Way duties. 9000 Class 'Dukedog' 4-4-0 No. 9011 sits in the 'Down' platform at Chipping Sodbury carrying a Class K headlamp code. Her driver looks back as if she is making a reverse manoeuvre. In the middle of the decade she was allocated to Swindon (82C) and by this stage in her career was reduced to light duties. She does not appear to have strayed very far from Swindon; out-shopped from the Works in March 1937 and allocated to the shed there. After twenty years service she was withdrawn from the same shed in July 1957, thus dating the photograph to the middle of the decade. These engines were Collett rebuilds of an earlier design, incorporating a boiler from the former 'Duke' Class with 'Bulldog' frames, intended for duties on light lines. They were one of the last classes of steam locomotive to have outside frames. Originally intended to carry the names of 'Earls', (see image 83) the idea was soon dropped when those personages objected to their names being carried by old fashioned locomotives with such a Victorian appearance. GH322.

Image 94, opposite: Along the finely manicured 'Down' platform at Chipping Sodbury a member of the Buildings Department strolls back towards his kit which appears to be strewn around the platform seat beneath the canopy. With piping and hacksaw in hand he glances at a Collett 'Grange' 68xx Class No. 6805 'Broughton Grange' thundering past on the 'Up' through road. The driver is also staring at the platform rather than the way ahead! From November 1952 to December 1957 '6805' was a Swindon based engine after which she was sent to work in Cornwall. With a Class 'A' express headcode being displayed it suggests the engine may have been standing in for something larger which had become unavailable. Note how pristine everywhere looks; not a weed to be seen either on the tracks or the platform. GH952.

Image 95, this page:: A trio of Chipping Sodbury train spotters are delighted to see a 'Castle' rushing east through the station on an 'Up' express. Carrying a blank reporting number frame on the smoke box door, partially obscuring the number plate, all that can be said is it is one of the '40xx' series. The photograph is a perfect late 1950s timepiece, when happy afternoons in school holidays were spent passing away the time of day on a country station platform. Closer inspection of the platform reveals all the usual paraphernalia, from staff/ passenger bicycles to barrow and platform trolleys. It is difficult to believe by 1960 only three 'Down' trains and two 'Up' trains called at the station each weekday. GH965.

Image 96: A picture probably taken from the signal box and definitely in a different season. Like all dedicated photographers George took his pictures in all kinds of weather. This shot was taken on a sunny winter morning at Chipping Sodbury. Skating through a vitrified landscape a gleaming 'Castle' heads east at the head of the 'Up' 'Capitals United Express'. This train, the 8am from Cardiff actually originated at 6.30am with through coaches from Swansea. It ran non-stop from Newport to Paddington where it was due at 10.50am. Seats could be reserved in advance for the princely sum of 2/- (10p) per seat. A Restaurant car was available throughout its journey. The 'Capitals United Express', although previously timetabled, was finally given the title in 1956 and lasted through to 1963. **GH970.**

Image 97: A panoramic view of Chipping Sodbury from the west. A beautifully presented Cardiff (Canton) (86C) 'Britannia' shatters the mid-morning calm as it storms through its tranquil setting with the 'Up' 'Red Dragon'. The Goods yard looks busy and is full of a variety of freight wagons. Is that the steam of the 'pick-up goods' engine shunting the yard, beyond the Goods shed roof? Standing in the 'Up' goods loop adjacent to the goods shed with its 'toad' brake van in the rear, is the stock of the train it may have temporarily deserted. 'The Red Dragon' had left her last call, Newport, at 10.20am so it must by now be about time for 'a brew' on the footplate of the express. Perhaps the crew of the goods train will be doing likewise. (The first coach behind the locomotive's tender appears to be one of the final variations of a Churchward 57ft Brake/ Third Class design dating back to the 1920s. The second coach is of the following generation; a Collett design of 1936 with large windows to each compartment. By now these would have been painted in the corporate colours of **BR**: described as Crimson Lake and Cream, more commonly 'Blood and Custard'. It also helps date the picture to the first half of the decade after the introduction of the 'Britannias' but prior to the overall phasing in of **BR** Mark 1 rolling stock.) **GH1008.**

Image 98, opposite: 'Still life'? George had the ability to capture the nuances of railway life as exemplified in this photograph at Chipping Sodbury. By taking a picture of silent sentinels he did, at the same time, wittingly or unwittingly capture another aspect of working life on the railway, or indeed, any other working environment of the period; the 'tea break'. This picture was taken at the same time as the 'Up' local goods train was sitting in the loop whilst shunting the yard. Look closely; beyond the 'Up' starter signals three men can be seen each heading in the same direction. They are bound for the Goods Yard 'Bothy'. In the bothy the kettle would have been simmering on the stove throughout the morning waiting for the moment when the teapot was to be filled. These three could easily have been the crew off the local goods; a guard and two loco men. Or one could have been the foreman or station porter. Whoever they were, they are about to join for a communal drink of tea. No doubt from the same kettle, billy-cans would be filled to be taken back to the footplate before the 'Up' Goods resumed its journey. Note also the Goods Yard 'privy'; the small shack seen between the foremost signal and its ladder. **GH960.**

Image 99, above: Moving a few hundred yards further west, another instance of George's ability to place a train into the landscape; who else would take a photograph of the tail end of a train going away from the camera? Yet this is something George did a number of times. It is a picture taken with an artist's perspective depicting a passing train as being 'Just a glimpse and gone forever' before disappearing into the distance. But George further illustrates his picture by using the smoke drifting up out of cottage chimneys and the skeletal trees bereft of leaves to tell us this is a view from winter or early spring. A 'Britannia' heads towards the station and will soon dive into Sodbury Tunnel with an eleven coach Paddington bound express from South Wales. **GH963.**

Image 100: Wapley Common and the surrounding areas, between Chipping Sodbury and Westerleigh were another of George's favoured locations; no doubt due to the range of opportunities the geography afforded. Here he is on the Downs at Wapley on a splendid evening as a 'Castle' with the eight coach formation of the 'Up' 'South Wales Pullman' rushes through. This train left Newport at 6.20pm so the time is probably just after seven o'clock as it was due at Paddington at 8.45pm. The exhaust from the locomotive's chimney shrouds Wapley Common Signal Box which can be seen behind the second coach. Like its counterpart at Westerleigh East Junction, which can just be seen in the distance, this signal box was a wartime build in 1942. Its purpose was to control operations to Wapley Common Sidings seen on the right. These were one of a number of such facilities constructed to serve the military as an Inland Sorting Depot and intended to relieve pressure on the ports, in this case specifically Avonmouth. With the closure of the Yard in 1965 the signal box became redundant and was closed. Wapley Box had one regular signalman by name of Alan Flook who worked the box from 1949 to 1965. During this period it was open from 6am on Monday mornings to 7pm on Sunday evenings. GH1093.

Image 101: An interesting picture for two reasons, the first is the locomotive at the head of the 'Down' 'Capitals United Express' and seen here drifting down the 1 in 300 past Westerleigh East Junction Signal Box. From what can be viewed through the frame work of the Train Reporting Number, the smoke box plate looks suspiciously like '6010'. That being so the engine is 'King Charles I'. But what is a 'King' doing on a South Wales Express? They were designed to handle the heaviest and fastest crack Great Western expresses on the Paddington to Plymouth and Paddington to Wolverhampton routes. The majority of them were based, as this one, at Old Oak Common (81A). However, towards the end of the decade they were being displaced from their old haunts by the diesels and some instead took up duties to South Wales. Indeed, by the time of withdrawal in June 1962, No. 6010 had become a Cardiff (Canton) based engine. A further point of interest are the two signal boxes. Both were built in 1942 to a wartime design intended to be more resilient to blast damage. Together they controlled the access and egress to the reception roads of Wapley Sidings. They were only 30 chains (660yds) apart and as such may have been some of the closest to each other on any main line. GH1161.

Image 102: A terrific view of No. 5083 'Bath Abbey', carrying a Class 'C' headlamp code, thundering through Westerleigh with a heavy milk train. You can almost feel the ground tremble as the tankers clank past; Westerleigh East Signal Box can just be glimpsed beyond the overbridge. This would very likely be empty milk tanks from Kensington Olympia to Fishguard. Because of the perishable nature of the consignment this kind of train was possibly the only sort of freight which ran to a passenger train schedule. In order to maintain the timings a 'Castle' would regularly be used. During the post-war austerity years, and throughout the decade following, it cannot be over emphasised how important milk was to the general well being of the nation. The average shipping distance by rail for milk was 250 miles and on the Western Region the two main trains to London were from Long Rock at Penzance and the 'Up' counterpart to this train. Between them they shipped 70,000,000 imperial gallons annually amounting to 25% of the country's total milk shipment. GH409.

Image 103: On the other side of the overbridge; another version of 'the perishables'. 'Hall' Class 4-6-0 No. 5963 'Wimpole Hall' heads east past Westerleigh East Junction Signal Box, the engine also displaying a Class 'C' headlamp code. This code denoted a 'parcels, fish, fruit, livestock, milk or other perishable train composed entirely of vehicles conforming to coaching stock requirements'. It also applied to an express freight, livestock, or ballast train, pipe-fitted throughout with the automatic vacuum brake operative on not less than half the vehicles piped to the engine. So it appears we are looking at the former with vans of fruit or other perishables coming up from the West Country or Wales potentially bound for London. In 1955 '5963' was based at Carmarthen (87G) but by February 1956 she was at Westbury (82D) so we are none the wiser. By 1953 Westerleigh East Box was switched out of circuit but in 1956, it reopened again between 5.30am and 4pm, Monday to Friday. On Saturdays it was from 6am to 2pm and on Sundays just 'as required'. The line in the foreground was the westerly entrance to Wapley Siding reception roads, by this time very rarely used. GH676.

Image 104: Silent Sentinels. Here George has taken his inspiration for this photograph not so much from the train as the infrastructure that supported it. A 'Castle' speeds past the camera with the 'Up' 'Bristolian'. The photographer relies on mood to bring his picture to life. The clouds darken as the sun goes down, its remaining rays lighting the train. It is framed by the original Great Western junction signal at Westerleigh East, the right arm of which was dismantled when the junction was taken out of use in 1950 after closure of the Westerleigh east to north curve. The drunken telegraph poles carry a multitude of complex information between signal boxes and other operational centres of the railway district. Is it the evening of the day or is it the sun going down on steam? GH1163.

Image 105: We are now approaching the other end of the triangle and Westerleigh West Junction. This time he captures BR 'Britannia' No. 70027 'Rising Star'. With steam feathering from the safety valves she appears to be coasting; midway down the thirteen miles long falling gradient from Badminton to Patchway. Out-shopped from Crewe Works in October 1952 she went direct to Cardiff (Canton) (86C) remaining there until December 1961 when she moved to the Midlands at Aston (21D). At Canton she spent much of her time plying her trade between Cardiff and Paddington together with the North and West route expresses to Shrewsbury. Train 'No.169' was first introduced into the timetable in the summer of 1952 as the 1.55pm Paddington to Neyland. From the 1953 timetable it became a weekday working. Then from summer 1955 the train's destination was changed to Pembroke Dock. This continued until the end of the summer 1957 timetable. Did George deliberately blur the image to give the impression of speed? GH140.

Image 106: A 'King' bound for London. The feature that makes this picture is the effect the dark towering cumulonimbus clouds create in accentuating the steam issuing from the engine's chimney. It evokes the sense of power as the locomotive speeds her train through the countryside. The unidentified 'King' heads 'The Red Dragon' east through the Westerleigh area displaying Train Reporting Number 'A35'. Pictured passing the 'Down' West Junction distance signal on the opposite side of the track, she is already well into the 1 in 300 climb to Badminton. As previously mentioned these Reporting Numbers were totally revised for the 1960 summer timetable introducing a letter into the code. The letter 'A' informs us the train is heading for Paddington and 'A35' can thus be identified as the weekday 7.30am Carmarthen to Paddington, the 'Up' 'Red Dragon'. This being a morning photograph the day doesn't bode well for further photography or those whose work involves being outside. GH1302.

Image 107: A Canton 'Britannia' No. 700023 'Venus' makes haste past Westerleigh Junction with Train No. '735'. In the summer of 1956 this number was allocated to the 8am Neyland to Paddington, which ran on summer Saturdays only and would have been passing this point at about one o'clock. It remained the same for the following summer seasons in 1957 and 1958. By 1959 the Reporting Number had been re-designated to become the weekday 18.55hrs. Paddington to Fishguard Harbour. So with the train in this picture travelling east we may conclude the view was taken sometime between 1956 and 1958. Made up to twelve coaches it was likely to have had portions from Fishguard Harbour and Pembroke Dock added en route. 'Venus' was released from Crewe Works in August 1951 and sent to Old Oak Common before finding her way to Canton. This is the kind of train these locomotives were built for; she appears to be climbing the 1 in 300 towards Badminton effortlessly. Westerleigh West Junction Signal Box can just be glimpsed behind the rear coach. GH128.

Image 108, this page: Another unidentified 'King' glides gracefully through Westerleigh Junction with a westbound train proudly proclaiming to be 'F64'. The GWR was the leading proponent of Train Reporting Numbers introducing them as far back as 1934. From the start of the summer service in June 1951 the Western Region reorganised these in order to achieve a better grouping of numbers. As the number of additional trains increased through the decade, particularly at weekends, further changes were made leading to a total revision for the Winter Timetable in 1958. Post 1960 the letter represented the shed code area in which the train's destination was located; the letter 'F' indicating the Cardiff and Swansea Districts. The number '64' was not a regularly used number in this series so, alas, it is not possible to say exactly where the train was bound. By this time West Junction had become Westerleigh Junction. GH1269.

Image 109, opposite top: A 'Castle' speeds its Paddington bound express east across Westerleigh Viaduct. The picture is taken from the former Midland main line from Bristol to Gloucester via Mangotsfield, just north of Westerleigh village. In it George demonstrates that the sky and features of the landscape framing the train are equally as important as the train itself. It is once again another example of 'a train in the landscape' with wispy cirrus clouds sweeping across the summer sky and a pastoral setting; in many respects the equivalent of a painted scene. The artist presses the shutter at precisely the right time, with the locomotive in the middle of the viaduct. The resulting picture speaks for itself. GH1279.

Image 110, this page, bottom: In this view, a 'Hall' Class 4-6-0 heads west over Westerleigh Viaduct; past the 'Upside' Westerleigh Junction Home signals. It is in charge of a mixed train of empty and loaded coal wagons probably heading for sorting at Stoke Gifford Yard. Below the viaduct the neat ballast shoulder and cess of the Midland route were typical of the period on both main line and lesser routes. The view is again taken from the south side of the viaduct on the Midland Main line to Yate and Gloucester. This was the former route of the Bristol and Gloucester Railway; ironically built by Isambard Kingdom Brunel to the broad gauge and opened in 1844. It was subsequently acquired by the Midland Railway and thereafter was in the vanguard of the battle between the broad and standard gauges. This was not resolved until 1872 when the Great Western converted all its broad gauge lines in the area to standard gauge. The connection here at Westerleigh between the GWR and MR subsequently led to further disputes between the two companies, each of whom would adopt delaying tactics applied to each other's workings. GH1286.

Image 111: A stranger on the line. Why is this Western Region engine approaching Westerleigh Viaduct on the former Midland route from Bristol rather than on the lines that run above it? 4900 'Hall' Class No. 6942 'Eshton Hall' has just passed Westerleigh village heading north with her Class 'D' express freight. From various other widespread locations throughout the earlier part of the decade, in September 1958, it was posted to Cardiff (Canton) (86C) for two months. From there it went to Old Oak Common (81A), on 1st November 1958, before moving back to South Wales in August 1963. She finally went to Gloucester (Horton Road) (85B) in June 1964 from where she was withdrawn six months later. So, perhaps, this was one of its swansong duties. But where did the train originate? The most likely answer would be Bristol but still no reason as to why it has taken the Midland route. GH1376.

Image 112: Now this is what you might call a real 'train in the landscape', surely a composition in its own right. Under a sky full of towering cumulus clouds the train is miniaturised. The scene is Winterbourne Viaduct on the Badminton route and we are standing on the south side of the line looking from a lane at Pye Corner towards a train entering onto the viaduct heading west. It is therefore a 'down' train, and headed by a gleaming 'Castle' locomotive trailing a fine ribbon of smoke and steam behind it. With its unusual appearance, this ten coach train, made up to include some clerestory twelve wheeled carriages, is certainly out of the ordinary and is in fact the formation of the 'Royal Train'. Where it is heading, and who was on board, goodness knows. Whatever, George has succeeded in recording a superb picture of it. GH1063.

Image 113: Trains meet at Westerleigh.   A Canton 'Britannia' has just crossed the Midland Region mainline from Birmingham to Bristol at Westerleigh with the westbound 'Red Dragon' on a July evening in 1956. She is hauling a rake of coaches painted in crimson lake and cream livery, otherwise known as 'blood and custard', the fourth coach of which is the Restaurant Car. This was the first general livery, decided upon in 1948 after the nationalisation of the railways; and to be adopted by all regions. Meanwhile an eastbound freight hauled by a GW 28xx 2-8-0 is slogging its way up the bank to Badminton with a freight from South Wales. To record trains crossing like this was a rare opportunity and in this picture George could hardly have arranged it better. Image GH1290.

Image 114: And so to Stoke Gifford Yard; looking west with neat lines of contemporary freight stock. Coal wagons predominate and there are two Great Western Toad Brake vans in the foreground. A bogie-bolster wagon loaded with a consignment of what appears to be flat-bottomed rails stands next to one of them. The code for such a wagon was a 'Macaw'. On an adjacent siding are eleven flat wagons each with a 'jeep' on board. At the time the military was a great customer of the railways. On the through line races an unidentified 'Castle' at the head of Train '460', the 11.45am Bristol (Temple Meads) – Paddington, running via the Badminton route. This service had been a fixture in the Western Region timetable throughout the decade; but from 1952 to 1955 running as a Saturdays only extra. From 1956 it was increased to a Weekday extra but in the 1959 revision of numbers it became Train '036'. With the changes in 1960 it then became Train 'A43' running on the two-hour schedule being due at Paddington at 1.45pm GH845.

Image 115: Skirting Bristol to the north we have travelled via Filton Junction and arrived at Patchway where George took this fine action shot. The contrast in the photograph is just right and the steam stands out against a clear sky. An express for South Wales, headed by a Canton 'Star'; **NOT** the original **GW** design but the more modern 'Britannia' **C**lass No. 70023 'Venus'. She appears to be opening up, possibly after a signal check, given that she is now on level track after the thirteen mile descent from Badminton. She carries the framework of a reporting number on the smoke box door but alas it remains blank so we can only guess what the destination may be. Notice all the whitening applied on the platform edge that has dribbled over the side. This whitening was put on using a small right-angle broom so the application lacked any finesse. It had originated during war time as an aid during the black out. However, the unanswered question is what is the train on the 'Up' line; no brake van and no tail lamp? Possibly a shunt move waiting for the down line to clear. GH940.

Image 116: **A** superb action view at the western end of Newport station in 1956. It may have been seen before but it is worth repeating as it incorporates all the business of the railways in the middle of the decade. The 'Paddington, Newport, Cardiff and Swansea' express, as the coach roof boards inform us, is the 8.55am Paddington-Neyland pulling out of the station past us and entering Hillfield Tunnel. To enable this to happen two short freight trains have been put into the 'Down' refuge sidings to allow its passage. One appears to consist of no more than an aged pannier tank, two open wagons and a 'Toad' brake van, whilst the other according to its signal has more recently arrived. However it is facing in the wrong direction so must have been' put inside' for an approaching passenger train. The '94xx' 0-6-0 pannier tank No. 8499 is an Ebbw Junction (86A) engine and would, according to her headlamp code, appear to be on an 'Up' pick-up freight. In the background a 0-6-2 tank runs bunker first out of the tunnel with coal wagons from the Valleys. **GH217.**

Image 117: Having now arrived at Cardiff we witness a busy scene beside Canton shed. From the look of her exhaust 'Grange' Class No. 6838 'Goodmoor Grange' has just been 'given the road' as she begins her journey from Cardiff General west with her 'Down' six coach stopping train. During the second part of the 1950s, having moved up from Laira to South Wales in August 1956, '6838' was based at Neyland (87H) for two months. She then went to Ebbw Junction (86A) where she remained until November 1961. So we may likely deduce this shot was taken in 1956 during her stay at Neyland. The Grange class was designed during the tenure of Mr. Collett at Swindon and first introduced in 1936. They were a variation of the 'Halls' with smaller wheels incorporating certain parts of withdrawn '4300' 2-6-0 locomotives. As with the 'Halls', the 'Granges' were rated as Class 5 mixed traffic engines. In the foreground one of her cousins, 'Hall' No.4926 'Farleigh Hall' is just coming on to the shed. Beyond, another No. 5901 'Hazel Hall' shielding a third behind her, takes refuge amongst carriages. GH157.

Image 118: Another very interesting picture at Canton. The shed was on the south side of the main line, 30 chains (660 Yards) from Cardiff West Signal Box, at the General Station. There was a footbridge here in front of the steam shed giving access to the Depot across the main lines and leading from a nearby street, which was intended for the use of railwaymen. But it was also the ideal place for photographers and train spotters; although I am sure the latter would have been discouraged. An interesting feature of the scene is the notice displayed on the hut in the left foreground which reads, "The Footbridge leading to Decrouche (*sic*) Place is the only proper way for workmen coming to and leaving duty. Any men disregarding this rule will be liable to dismissal". George took a series of photographs here in 1956, including the previous view. In this image looking west from the footbridge the prominent Signal Box is Canton Sidings and past it races a westbound passenger train on the South Wales main line headed by a 'Castle'. In the foreground coming on to shed is '4900 Hall' Class No. 6994 'Baggrave Hall' which featured in other previously published Heiron photographs. From April 1954 to November 1961 she was based at Westbury (82D) so her duty here may well have been working a train of empty coal wagons back to South Wales. GH 280.

Image 119: In another view from the same footbridge spanning the numerous tracks outside the shed at Canton; we see two footplate men make their way across the lines. Perhaps they have come from the 'County' Class No. 1022 'County of Northampton', the cab of which looks deserted. They may be looking for their relief; 'Western' loco. men were renowned for looking for their 'Grub, Water and Relief' (GWR)! As with 'Baggrave Hall' in the previous photograph, No. 1022 is visiting from Westbury (82D). In front of her, on one of the carriage roads stands a 'Hall' 4-6-0. The grimy '5700' Class Pannier tank No. 3755 is a long standing Cardiff based workhorse and in the foreground we catch glimpses of two BR 'Standard' 4-6-0's, the boiler of one and the tender of another. As with the previous photograph this was one of the series taken by George at Canton in 1956. GH174.

Image 120: The smell of the acrid sulphurous smoke surrounding the shed is almost palpable. This picture is so reminiscent of many a steam shed up and down the country; you could almost cut the atmosphere with a knife. Whilst it was home to a number of express passenger locomotives Canton was principally a freight engine depot. George has captured a number of such engines here with a BR 9F 2-10-0 No. 92222 prominent in the foreground. This engine was not delivered from Crewe Works until June 1958 so this must have been on a subsequent visit by George to Canton. Out of two hundred and fifty one such locomotives built, it was in the last batch of thirty. But here her grimy condition is already apparent. This engine had a short working life of only just less than seven years, being withdrawn in March 1965. It was subsequently scrapped. It is carrying a Banbury (84C) shed plate where it was first allocated and has probably worked in with a freight off the Great Central lines and thence via Swindon. Also prominent are three ex WD 'Austerity' Class 9F locomotives including the tender of one in the bottom left hand corner. Of the two which can be identified No.90201 was based at Canton from March 1955 to March 1961. In the background, No. 90507 is visiting from Woodford Halse (2F) on the ex-Great Central so has probably performed a similar duty to No. 92222. By 1959 Woodford Halse, formerly (38E) had been redesignated as 2F. GH172.

Image 121: Canton again but this time we are in the carriage sidings. 'Modified Hall' No.7912 'Little Linford Hall' threads its way through. The Driver stares diligently ahead and with the engine having steam to spare the fireman stands with his hands clasped behind his back. '7912' was built well into BR days, being out-shopped from Swindon in March 1950. Throughout the decade she was based at Tyseley (84E), apart from two months at Shrewsbury during 1955, so she could be on a through working from the north west. The coaching stock on display is a complete cross-section of that produced throughout the Great Western period. A Churchward bow-ended 'toplight' designed in 1922 is on the far road with the roof of another in the foreground. Collett developments featuring wider windows from 1936 can also be seen as well as Hawksworth produced bow-roofed stock introduced from 1944. A 'Prairie' Tank hides itself between the first bow-ended coach of the train and the stock beyond. This could be the yard shunter or more likely the Cardiff General pilot engine. GH387.

Image 122: Interlude at Cardiff (Queen Street). A BR Derby 'Lightweight' Diesel Multiple Unit forming a train off the Valley Lines drifts into the station. It is not so much about the train in this composition as all the other aspects that come together to make a complete picture. A porter is slumped against a storage box with 'fag in hand'; has he had a liquid lunch? Then there is a young boy in short trousers recording details of the DMU. And we have another man, quite possibly a railwayman, adopting a hand on hip, 'what time do you call this?' pose. Also of interest are the posters of the period representing such diverse subjects as the *Western Mail* newspaper, Huntley & Palmer's Biscuits, Walpamur Paints and even a recruiting poster for the Metropolitan Police featuring a 'Dixon of Dock Green' character. GH166.

Image 123, top: The east end of Cardiff General Station just before 10am on a summer Saturday morning in 1958. In the main 'Up' platform sits 'The Red Dragon' behind No. 70018 'Flying Dutchman'. This train originated at Carmarthen at 7.30am and was due to leave Cardiff at 10am. 1958 was the first year it was designated Train '726' the reporting number it carried throughout the week. Why it was necessary to carry this boldly displayed number as well as a commanding headboard, for a signalman to recognise which train it was, is a matter of conjecture. At the adjacent platform sporting a much more understated reporting number '770' stands a 'Hall' No. 6943 'Farnley Hall'. She is in charge of the 10.08am (SO) Cardiff to Portsmouth Harbour. For the three previous years this train had run to Portsmouth and Southsea only but had now been extended for the benefit of holiday makers bound for the Isle of Wight. GH161.

Image 124, bottom: A classic South Wales view on the eastern outskirts of Cardiff; as we begin our journey back to Temple Meads. This picture brings together coal and steam, both part of the same umbilical cord. On the railway, steam was to coal as coal was to steam. Here the statement is harmonised at Pengam Junction Signal Box. 'Hall' No. 6927 'Lilford Hall' bearing train reporting number, '737' heads what must have been a hastily arranged train since its number does not appear in subsequently compiled lists. George records it as a 'Devon-bound Saturday special, clattering its way east through the Pengam Yards". During the latter part of the decade No. 6927 was an Oxford (81F) allocated engine and before that had spent five years at Reading (81D). But during peak traffic on summer Saturdays a locomotive could be pressed into service by whichever shed it happened to have arrived at. Meanwhile to the left of the picture a 94xx Pannier Tank runs bunker first behind the Signal Box down the Roath Dock Branch line, with a train of pulverised coal, under the watchful eye of a trilby-hatted official. GH296.

Image 125: Approaching Newport and an all encompassing railway scene. Miles of sidings holding hundreds of coal wagons brought down from the valleys. Coal is again at the forefront. Through a myriad of lines at Alexandra Dock Junction 'Castle' No. 7014 'Caerhays Castle' threads its way past the Signal Box with an 'Up' ten coach stopping train. This was the 5.23pm semi-fast from Cardiff to Bristol Temple Meads. No. 7014 was a Bath Road based engine. Waiting patiently behind the Signal Box a well presented 'Hall' No. 4913 'Baglan Hall', a Canton engine, waits for a path with its eastbound coal train. The picture is taken, quite possibly from Maesglas Junction Signal Box, which controlled the freight lines from Park Junction and the Western Valleys into the main Newport Docks, spanning the South Wales Main Line at this point. In the middle distance is the Western Loop from Park Junction and the Valleys carrying the freight lines into Alexandra Docks. The signal box on this line, above the locomotive, is West Mendalgief Junction, which controlled access to the sidings of the same name and located to its left. Interest in the background is provided by Uskmouth Power Station. This was opened in the early 1950s and demolished in 2002. Beyond, a ship navigates the River Usk on its way into Newport Docks. GH179.

Image 126, opposite top: From almost the same point, but in this case viewed in the opposite direction, we are looking at Gaer Junction just west of Hillfield Tunnel, the other end of which opens out into the western throat of Newport Station. On the left of the picture a three-car BR Class 108 'Derby Suburban' (later Class 116) DMU drifts towards the tunnel and its destination at Newport. These units were introduced in 1958 to replace aged steam stock and provided a service to the Sirhowy and Ebbw Valleys from Newport. In the foreground also heading east is a heavy goods train, again loaded with pulverised coal on the 'Up' relief line. It is being held at the Gaer Junction home signal just in front of the signal box. Note the plethora of signals dotted around the box, from which it can be deduced that westbound trains are expected on both the 'Down' main line and the 'Down' relief. The scene today bears little resemblance to this neat and tidy aspect. GH197.

Image 127, opposite bottom: A summer shot at Newport and yes schoolboys did wear school uniform on Saturdays in the 1950s! Many working class lads didn't have a great deal else to change into. The platform clock shows the time to be 12.40pm as No 70025 'Western Star' runs in with a heavy passenger train. No. 70025 was based at Canton from May 1953 to September 1961 when she became displaced by the increasing introduction of diesel power on to the Western Region. She is carrying a Train Reporting Number frame on her smoke box door but annoyingly it is blank. In his book, 'Roaming the Western Rails' George records this scene taken in 1955 as '*a twelve coach train from Carmarthen to Paddington with two restaurant cars*' but it is difficult to identify them in the picture. Without the relevant timetable of the period it is also difficult to identify which train it would be. The fireman gazing out of his cab window certainly looks very unconcerned. If it is summer it is certainly a cool one, all the passengers have either a coat or jacket on. In their minds the old anxieties will be there; will we get a corner seat to ourselves or have to share our compartment with someone else? GH190.

Image 128, above: Back under the Severn Tunnel a highly polished and resplendent '70xx' series 'Castle', with burnished buffers, is at grips with the 1 in 80 gradient out of the eastern end of Patchway tunnel. Note the smoke haze lingering around the tunnel mouth. The train, the 'South Wales Pullman', had been climbing continuously for six miles from half-way through the Severn Tunnel and would so continue almost unbroken for another fourteen miles to Badminton. The 'South Wales Pullman' was introduced in 1955 and was due to commence service on 13th June, at the beginning of the summer timetable. However, due to a strike by **ASLEF** it did not start until Monday 27th June. Meals and refreshments were served at every seat and there was also an attractive bar called the 'Daffodil'. Leaving Swansea at 4.30pm the train called at Port Talbot, Cardiff and Newport before running fast to Paddington where it was due to arrive at 8.45pm. In 1961 the service became a Blue Pullman (an 8-car diesel multiple unit) which continued until 1973 when the Pullman service was withdrawn. GH938.

Image 129: Having forked right at Filton Junction we come to a location which gave George the opportunity to take arresting action photographs. This was the four and a half mile climb from Dr. Day's Bridge Junction up to Filton Junction; hard work for an engine and its crew. At Ashley Down under a mackerel sky, a Hawksworth '10xx' 'County' 4-6-0 No. 1026 'County of Salop' is at grips with the bank, coming out of Narroways Hill Cutting. With a chimney exuding plumes of steam the fireman must have been working overtime shovelling coal for all he was worth. From October 1955, No. 1026 became a Shrewsbury (84G) based locomotive and in 1958 was fitted with a double chimney. So this may well be a West to North express sometime between those three years. Given the low sun in the western sky glinting off the boiler in autumn, this could well be the 1.10pm Plymouth-Manchester, due away from Temple Meads around 5.25pm. Note the second vehicle behind the tender. This is a GWR Centenary Saloon designed by Charles Collett in 1935. These twenty six carriages were a development of the eight 'Super Saloons' built for the Ocean Liner traffic from Plymouth to Paddington earlier in 1931. Their use was specifically for the 'Cornish Riviera Express' although some twenty years later were now absorbed into the general rolling stock pool. GH906.

Image 130: At much the same location, another West to North express, this time in the charge of an unidentified 'Castle' and displaying a Train Reporting Number '285'. This number first appeared in the summer of 1955 referring to the 10.05am Penzance-Liverpool which would indicate this was either a Newton Abbot or Shrewsbury based locomotive. From the winter timetable 1955/6 the train had been moved back and originated at Plymouth as the 1.10pm to Liverpool. This process continued until the winter of 1958 when the trains for both seasons became a permanent fixture in the timetable. During this period there was a 'double home' duty for footplate crew on the service alternating between Shrewsbury and Newton Abbot men. The Shrewsbury crew would work down on the 9.5am Liverpool (11.18am ex Shrewsbury), Salop Turn 102, and lodge overnight at Newton Abbot and then return home the following day on the ex- Penzance service such as this; vice versa the Newton Abbot crew, Turn 154. Very fit men would be required! GH912.

Image 131: Bearing the lifelines of communication on the railway system in steam days; a tangle of telegraph poles. Gazing out of a carriage window the continuous line of sagging wires between poles was always a feature of any journey. Here George has crafted a picture using his artistic eye to frame the trains between the drunken poles. He is standing on top of Ashley Down looking south through Narroways Cutting to an industrial north Bristol landscape beyond. In the foreground the quadruple Western Region lines are spanned by the Midland line from Kingswood Junction to Ashley Hill Junction and Avonmouth. Beneath, on the slow line a very heavy coal train trundles cautiously down the bank towards Stapleton Road. Overtaking the freight is a Temple Meads bound passenger train in the hands of what appears to be a 'Hall' or 'Grange'. In the distance more steam is at work and there is a general haze shrouding the suburbs. Whilst it might not be the most arresting picture, it is nevertheless very well composed and ably illustrates the industrial side of railway operations. **GH1072.**

Image 132, top: An industrial landscape in all its desolation; nothing but power and grime dominate the scene at Stapleton Road Junction on the 1 in 75 climb out of Bristol to Filton. Dominated by the huge gasometer a '42xx' 2-8-0T No. 5236 battles its way up the bank, with grateful assistance in the rear from an unidentified engine, hauling its heavy 'H' Class unfitted freight. Being a Newport (Ebbw Junction) (86A) allocated locomotive it may be safe to assume that its train is headed for South Wales. It is passed in the 'Down' direction by another freight headed by what appears to be a '43xx' Class engine, gently descending the bank. With the vans at the front, this train may well be partly fitted with the vacuum brake. Little wonder then that her safety valves are blowing as she cautiously drops down into Bristol. Since 1878 Eastville had been home to the Bristol Gas Company which had two gasometers on their site adjacent to the railway at this point. There was always a pervading smell of gas in the vicinity so a holiday in the caravan in the yard on the right hand side of the picture was not to be recommended! GH443.

Image 133, bottom: Taken from much the same position and quite possibly on the same day beside the towering trackside gas holder, ex-Great Western '63xx' 2-6-0 No. 6363, a St. Phillip's Marsh (82B) allocated engine, is working hard at the rear of a heavy freight train. It is assisting up the bank to Filton Junction and probably Stoke Gifford Yard. Meanwhile an unidentified 'Hall' begins the descent towards Temple Meads with a down passenger train. The lines to the right lead off to Clifton Down and Avonmouth Docks joining the Midland line from Kingswood junction at Ashley Hill Junction. Despite Dr. Beeching's best efforts the passenger service along this route to and from Severn Beach has survived. Since that time suburban traffic in the Bristol area has increased enormously to the point that there are now 25 trains per day along the route whilst 120,000 people annually were reported to have used Avonmouth station in 2014-15. GH1069.

Image 134, above: Just a little further south but in total contrast to the previous two pictures, a shot that captures the quiet atmosphere of a small suburban junction station. As its running-in board proudly proclaims Stapleton Road was the 'Junction for South Wales, Clifton and Avonmouth'. Indeed during this time some mainline passenger trains avoiding a necessary reversal at Temple Meads, stopped here where passengers travelling west via the main station were obliged to change in order to reach their destination. Principal amongst these were some of the through services between South Wales and the South Coast running via Westbury and Salisbury. However, in this case, we see '5100' Class 2-6-2T No. 5188, drifting down Filton Bank and into the station with a four coach train of suburban stock. No. 5188 was a local Bristol engine from August 1957 spending short spells at both Bath Road and St. Phillips Marsh sheds before being transferred to Newport (Ebbw Junction) (86A) in May 1958. It was withdrawn from there in July 1962. The somewhat unkempt machine displays a Class B headlamp code. The shadows suggest the train may be an afternoon or evening stopper perhaps from Newport to Temple Meads. With the starting signal on the left being set in the 'off' position, it appears an Avonmouth bound train is expected. GH1081.

Image 135, opposite: Taken by a cameraman with an artist's eye; a panoramic view looking south from Dr. Day's Bridge at the bottom of the bank. Passing the Junction Signal Box of the same name, we have a fine action shot of a northbound express being hauled by an unidentified '49xx' series 'Hall' 4-6-0. With the regulator fully open, she is taking a run at the four and a half miles climb to Filton Junction. No. '560' was the summertime 10.55am (SO) Ilfracombe to Birmingham throughout the decade from 1952 to 1957 whilst from 1958 the working was extended to Wolverhampton (Low Level) due to demand. Post 1959 it became No. '848' and with the complete overhaul of numbers for 1960 it was changed again to 'H28'. Dr. Days' Bridge was named after Dr. William Edward Day who lived in Barrow Road when the cutting was needed to be made to enable the railway to pass. On the loop to the left stands a short goods train headed by what appears to be a '72xx' 2-8-2T. GH763.

Image 136: Probably taken at much the same time as the previous picture, this shot encapsulates the whole railway scene; two trains, a tangle of tracks and an abundance of signals all sewn together by the signal box. From his open window the signalman dutifully scans the passing 'Castle' hauled express as it weaves its way the last few hundred yards towards Temple Meads. Meanwhile on the east to north loop a goods working has been brought to a stand at the stop signal in order to allow the passage of the passenger train. This curve was colloquially known as the 'Rhubarb Loop', the name taken from the Rhubarb Tavern on nearby Queen Anne Road. The goods, probably originating from Bristol East Yard, is headed by '28xx' No. 2858. The locomotive displays a headlamp code for a Class 'H', representing an unfitted through freight. From December 1954 No. 2858 was a South Wales based engine, first at Ebbw Junction (86A) and then Severn Tunnel Junction from where it was withdrawn in February 1963. This must give us a clue as to where this train was bound. GH761.

Image 137: And that, by a somewhat convoluted route, brings us back once more to Temple Meads where we look east from the rooftop of 'Hares Rainbow Paints' factory. A 'Grange' No. 6846 'Ruckley Grange', with the Train Reporting Number '703', hurriedly scrawled in chalk at the top of its smoke box door, pilots sister engine No. 6840 'Hazeley Grange' with their double headed train; clearly bolstered due to demand. They snake across the myriad of tracks past Bristol East Power Box. During this period both were based at primarily freight sheds, No. 6846 at St. Philip's Marsh (82B) and No. 6840 at Pontypool Road (86G) so both had been pressed into summer Saturday service on passenger duties. Train '703' was introduced as a summer Saturday extra in 1952 as the 8.10am (**SO**) Newport to Paignton. This was repeated each year until 1958 when its journey was stretched at each end to become the 8.05am Cardiff to Kingswear. The Power Box dates from 1935 when the Great Western Railway was still in its prime. Built in the Art Deco style it was the largest such box on the GWR with 363 levers, the GWR sticking to the 'one lever - one operation' rather than a power box with route setting capacity. (The exception was at Newport where a route setting frame had been installed in 1927.) Demolished in 1970 it was one of the Bristol boxes superseded by Multiple Aspect Signalling (**MAS**). GH1577.

Image 138: George has now turned his camera around to record a fine panorama at the east end of Temple Meads Station on a busy summer Saturday morning. On the left small Prairie No. 5553 (82A) stands adjacent to the loading bank with an assortment of vans. Meanwhile the well-loaded summer extra seen in the previous photograph runs into the picture towards Platform 3, double headed by the pair of 'Granges'. In front of them alongside Platform 6, with her safety valves blowing impatiently, is a 'Standard Class 5' with an 'Up' passenger train. Further across a 'Castle', blurred in its own exhaust, stands with another 'Up' train, and finally in Platform 9, a humble Pannier Tank heads two suburban coaches. This could well be the Avonmouth shuttle. The background is filled by the huge Western Region Goods Depot and on the extreme right a couple of coaches wait, according to George, to be added to the front of an incoming train. GH1569.

Image 139: So now we come to a nocturne at **Temple Meads**. 'Castle' **No. 5076 'Gladiator'** stands alongside Platform 9. The station is remarkably deserted; the only person to be seen is a man, who could well be a railway official, talking to the locomotive crew. Given that the clock on the opposite platform shows the time to be coming up to 6.25pm may indicate that it is a rather cold winter evening. If that were the case the train may well be the 4.35pm ex **Taunton** due to leave Bristol at 6.25pm for **Paddington**. It was allowed a leisurely three hours to complete the journey after putting in extended stops at all principal stations. We have seen previously how important to both the railways and what was then called the **General Post Office**, the conveyance of mail was and this could well be the reason for the easy schedule. Built in 1938, **No. 5076** was transferred from **Bath Road** to **Reading (81D)** in March 1960 and from there to **Old Oak Common** in May 1963. She was one of the later members of the **Castle** class to be withdrawn lasting until September 1964. **GH048.**

Image 140: The evening of steam is further marked by 'King' No.6026 'King John' in Platform 9 at Temple Meads with the same train, perhaps one of George's favourites. It is safe to assume this train carried a fairly large quantity of mail/ parcels as the service was due at Temple Meads at 6.13pm but allowed 12 minutes for loading/ unloading. A great deal of mail was always to be seen during the evenings at major railway stations, piled high on four wheeled barrows, as witnessed here, in the background on Platform 7. In 1959, as indicated by her shed plate, No. 6026 was a Plymouth Laira (83D) allocated engine whilst her previous almost exclusive express work was beginning to be taken over by diesel power. Hence duties were becoming limited. By February 1960 she had been transferred to Old Oak Common (81A) from where she was withdrawn in September 1962 and sent to Swindon in November 1963 for cutting up. GH1614.

Image 141: In a later view the transition from steam to diesel becomes marked. A friendly chat before departure between the driver and a father, or is he a grandfather - look at the polish on his shoes? Is he perhaps trying to get the children interested in trains? From the Platform 9 clock it appears to be approaching 6.15. The driver is in charge of a 'Western' Class Diesel Hydraulic No. D1006 'Western Stalwart' standing at the head of the train; note too the then requisite second-man in the offside seat of the cab. During the early days of dieselisation this was the title given to the former fireman although in reality he had little in the way of actual duties to perform. Overnight his job had changed from keeping the fire stoked and the boiler pressure up to ensuring the train-heat boiler was working, and the tea-can filled with sufficient for the journey. The 'Westerns' were first introduced in 1961; following on from the 'Warships' and so further displacing steam. A glance at the winter timetable 1962/63 shows the 4.47pm ex Taunton arrived at Temple Meads at 6.9pm and was due away at 6.15pm. The Letter 'A' in the reporting number indicates it is Paddington bound. Could this be the same working, slightly retimed, as in the previous pictures? **GH**1591.

Image 142, top: Seasons change and after all good summers autumn is bound to follow. In photographic terms and to illustrate the fact George truly was a 'Man for All Seasons', a poor weather view at the west end of Platform 4 at Temple Meads. In the background is Bath Road Depot but on the rain-soaked platform all the attention is focussed on the locomotive at the head of the train. This is BR 'Britannia' No 70023 'Venus' built at Crewe in 1951 and allocated to Old Oak Common (81A). By the interest she is receiving, to many people, the (steam) engine was still something of an innovation as they look on admiringly. The roof board on the leading coach shows the train to be a 'Paddington Exeter and Plymouth'. This raises the question 'what is this train doing at Bristol?' It could conceivably be a morning shot rather than an evening one. If the shed clock in the background is to be believed and read as about 8.37 then this could be the 5.30am from Paddington running via Bristol where it was due at 8.31am and timed to leave at 8.45am. This would be substantiated by the local train arriving at Platform 6 behind a Class '51xx' Tank engine that may be the 7am 'all-stations' from Taunton due at 8.38am. Certainly 'Venus' appears impatient to start and the stance of the young man, standing next to the leading carriage open window waiting to see off a lady, appears to be sharing that impatience. GH1107.

Image 143, bottom: Some steam workings lasted well into the 1960s but they became increasingly rare on the Western Region and were restricted to visitors from other Regions. This is a good example. Driver Eames on sister engine No. 70045 'Lord Rowallan' has just brought a Wolverhampton to Paignton summer holiday extra into Temple Meads and looks for the signal at the western end of Platform 5 before moving off to Bath Road shed. In the background a 'Hymek' runs off the shed, very likely to take the train onwards to Paignton. No. 70045 was based at Wolverhampton Oxley, (by then 2B) from the middle of June to early October 1965. During this period the locomotive worked several summer Saturday trains from Wolverhampton bound for both Penzance and Ilfracombe being relieved here at Bristol. Train spotters and enthusiasts were still numerous and the older ones amongst them show total disregard for the two notices prominently displayed at the platform end explicitly forbidding anyone to pass them. It has to be said the lower of the two notices refers to a barrier which must not be passed and yet there is no barrier. Clearly the young group of photographers at the bottom of the slope have taken licence from this! So who was 'Lord Rowallan' after whom the locomotive was named? In 1945, after a distinguished military career he became the Chief Scout of the British Commonwealth and Empire, a position he held until 1959. During the 1950s the Scouts was a very popular movement for young boys and to this day still remains 'a force for good'. GH1145.

Image 144: Steam has died. A panoramic view of Temple Meads station in the post steam age, taken from the west. Even so for the present the only part of the infrastructure that has changed is the replacement of the old steam shed at Bath Road by a gleaming new diesel depot on the upper right of the photograph. The water tank looks as if it is the only survivor. A 'Class 119' Gloucester Railway Carriage and Wagon Company three-car diesel multiple unit, in tandem with another, scurries from beneath the A4 overbridge and past Bristol West signal box. These units were introduced from 1960 and allocated to the Western Region. The train seems to be well filled except in the first-class compartment at the front. It appears to be a lovely summer day; hence the service may well be bound for Weston-super-Mare. GH1031.

Image 145: To conclude, another panorama of the west end of Temple Meads Station in the post-steam era; how things have changed. All the hustle and bustle has gone; steam has all but been eliminated and the atmosphere around Bath Road shed has lightened; it is now diesel fumes that are pervading the atmosphere rather than smoke and steam. From out of what appears to be a relatively deserted station, creeps a 'Warship' class Diesel No. D834 'Pathfinder', one of the thirty three 'Warships built by the North British Locomotive Company in Glasgow, a second series production of the original D800 series. They were ordered by the British Transport Commission (British Railways Board) but were not well received nor ever gained favour on the Western Region, hence they had a very short lifespan. Well into the 1950s, ten years after nationalisation, the Western Region still fiercely defended its heritage and much preferred its own Swindon built version. As is often the case, these NBLC locomotives were the product of power politics. Hence the short life and were outlived by many of their D800 (Swindon) counterparts. D834 was introduced into service on 26th July 1960 and withdrawn eleven years later on 3rd October 1971 being cut-up at Swindon in February of the following year. The head code shows the train to be '1B08'. With the letter 'B' indicating a destination in the Bristol District it is probably safe to assume the train is bound for Weston-super-Mare and where our journey had begun. GH1111.

Publishers note: Some of the George Heiron images seen on the preceding pages has been published previously. Although a full and comprehensive list is not available, George's work has appeared in 'Trains to the West', 'Roaming the Western Rails', 'Steam's Indian Summer', 'Trainspotter's Annual' and 'Trains Illustrated / Modern Railways'.